Iron Roads to the
BROADS & FENS

MICHAEL PEARSON

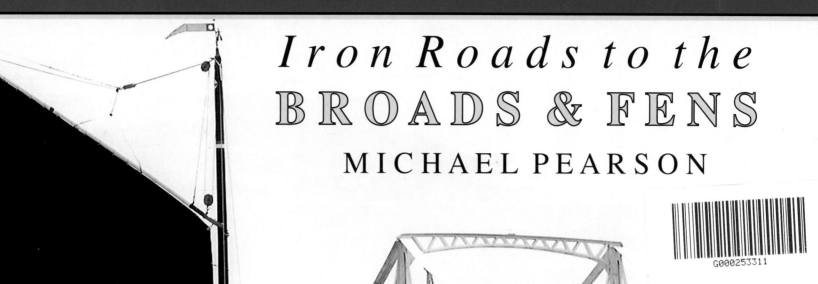

WAYZGOOSE

www.wayzgoose.org.uk Tel: 01283 713674/821472
Copyright: Michael Pearson All Rights Reserved
First Edition 2005 ISBN 0 9545383 7 4

Towards the melodramatic denouement of Alfred Hitchcock's 1938 screen version of *The Lady Vanishes*, the heroine (demurely played by Margaret Lockwood) asks the hero (a dashing Michael Redgrave) where they should go for their honeymoon? Emphatically he responds 'somewhere without any trains!' Considering the adventurous, trans-European railway journey they'd just endured - culminating in a dining-car shoot-out on a remote Ruritanian branch line - one can appreciate his prejudice, but it was not an outlook likely to appeal to my new wife and I on our Norfolk honeymoon in 1979.

Where *we* could we *went* by train. Unforgiveably, our beloved Wells-next-the-Sea had fifteen years earlier been severed from the system by the abhorrent Doctor, whose flawed vision had also terminated train services to Melton Constable and Mundesley-on-Sea. The coast road was one long line of impatiently snaking traffic, so we cut inland, coming upon as many abandoned stations as we did forgotten churches, drawing a moral somehow there, as if Britain's railways and the Anglican religion were both diminishing faiths.

So we were happier when we could go by rail, savouring a forward view over the avuncular shoulders of the drivers of Cravens or Metro-Cammell railcars. Watching crossing-keepers emerge unhurriedly from quaint weather-boarded lineside cottages to open level crossing gates with an unnerving sense of timing, honed by years of experience.

We indulged ourselves, but it was difficult not to come away with the impression that Norfolk's rural railways were hanging on by the skin of their neglected teeth. That many of the Beeching /Marples closures had been irrational, paradoxically inferred that the branch lines which had survived were themselves victims of myopic policy-making.

Two or three years later, when Alexander Frater travelled from Norwich to Sheringham to write a piece for *The Observer* (later anthologised into a book called *Stopping Train Britain*) he confessed that the 'country train was clearly a doomed species'. Paul Theroux, journeying contemporaneously round the coast of Norfolk for his travelogue, *The Kingdom by the Sea*. was forestalled by a railway strike, and met a man who averred that within a few years there would be no trains to King's Lynn, Cromer, Yarmouth or Lowestoft at all.

If Norfolk's railways had no future, they certainly had a past. These were the fiefdoms of the Great Eastern and the Midland & Great Northern railways whose locomotives were blue and yellow respectively. The Great Eastern was a huge concern, the Midland & Great Northern a jointly owned incursion born out of misplaced optimism, competition and rivalry.

To put them in focus you had to turn to that most lyrical of railway historians, Cuthbert Hamilton Ellis. In his opinion the Great Eastern was less changed by the amalgamations of 1923 than any other English railway; quite a claim when one considers that the Great Western sailed through the grouping unimpaired. But you could see what he meant, for in a sense it was the East Anglian landscape which shaped the GER - 'the old Great Eastern winding slow to some forgotten country town' as John Betjeman put it - and change has always been slow in permeating Britain's hindquarters.

To Hamilton Ellis, Great Eastern trains sported a colour scheme so rich as to resemble, variously, Victorian stained glass in a highly restored church, or the cookery of Tudor England. Why even the upholstery in third class was trimmed with turkey-red velvet. They were the first company to enliven compartment bulkheads with

framed photographs of interesting places served by its trains. In their carriages' clerestory decklights they mounted coloured transparencies of seaside resorts. Their best expresses exemplified pride and quality, and provided the most smartly served restaurant car dinners in the world. Against such stiff opposition, the Midland & Great Northern had its work cut out to achieve parity. But it had a wonderful guiding light in the shape of William Marriott who had a genius for railway management and saw to it that his company cashed in on the popularity of 'Poppyland'. In the rural wilds of North Norfolk, Melton Constable became the hub of the Midland & Great Northern network. A bucolic Crewe where long trains of impatient holidaymakers from the East Midlands were broken up and marshalled into independent portions for Sheringham & Cromer, Yarmouth & Lowestoft and Norwich.

Marriott was a marvel. The sort of man whose energies in another milieu might have been harnessed to propel a Third Division football club to the Cup Final. He ruled the M&GN like a benign autocrat, patenting a machine for making concrete from which was fashioned signal posts, cattle pens, platelayers huts and running-in boards. Alight at West Runton today - lovingly tended, with what amounts to maternal care, by the Womens Institute - and you will find one of Marriott's concrete nameboards still proclaiming your arrival a century on.

In the workshops at Melton Constable the M&GN maintained and occasionally built its own rolling stock and locomotives. A trio of 4-4-2 tank engines (designed, of course, by William Marriott) produced in the early years of the 20th century, were profitably employed until very nearly the end of the Second World War, and were as elegant as anything ever built by better known railways. During the First World War those same workshops were turned over to the production of munitions. Some firth-columnist must have got word back to Berlin, as Melton Constable was attacked by Zeppelins for its troubles.

One day we drove through Norfolk lanes in search of this railway Xanadu. The workers houses were still intact; incongruous northern terraces in what, on the surface of it, was a somnolent East Anglian village, whilst part of the works was in use as an industrial estate. But the most poignant manifestation of the long vanished railway was a bus shelter, supported by M&GN cast iron brackets, bearing a mural of one of Mr Marriott's lovely gorse coloured tank engines. A haunting image of a lost railway empire.

*　　*　　*

Time passed. We raised a family. On a snowy weekend we journeyed from Leicester to Norwich, putting up at the Maids Head. Our train consisted of four steam-heated bogie carriages dragged by an ageing diesel locomotive. We had a compartment to ourselves, as comfortable and as private as our own front parlour. The Shires and Fens and Brecks rolled past our wide window: Betjeman's 'Unmitigated England - swinging down the line'. This was the apothesis of travel. And yet the knives were still out. The Serpell Report, though subsequently rebuffed - more, I suspected, through inertia than scruple - suggested that there were still fifth columnists in the corridors of power who would gladly blood-let the bulk of our railway system. The reality was that the railways were a political pawn; dogma obfuscated their true value as a finite, environmentally sustainable, mode of transport. Rail's very limitations were its strengths. Sooner or
later road traffic raped and pillaged
everything from

the village green to the market square. A railway stopped in its tracks at the station or goods yard, leaving its hinterland unblemished and intact.

And so it became preferable to live in the past, to imagine that one could still reach Hunstanton, Swaffham, Dereham and Fakenham by rail. Ensconced in an armchair with old timetables, I would draw up whimsical itineraries, only too happy if the spare schedules of the past necessitated lengthy hiatuses; all the more imaginary time at my disposal to rummage through secondhand bookshops, lunch on bread and cheese and local beer in stone-flagged country inns, and wander by river banks where barges still plied, making their own uniquely demure contribution to transport. Earning my living compiling guide books, I had prematurely arrived at the awful realisation that England was being annihilated faster than I could track it down.

*   *   *

Even with the grossly overrated benefits of hindsight, it is difficult to put one's finger on the point at which Britain's rural railways began to flow as opposed to ebb. For a while it was like standing on a beach, trying to determine which way the tide was turning. In 1985 a personable young woman called Kerry Hamilton made a television series entitled *Losing Track*. It helped that she was young and female. Most proponents of the railway were middle aged and male, and therefore easily lampooned as anoraks. It is of course impossible to gauge accurately what impact her series had on the television-watching public, but it tentatively lifted the curtain, and its underlying message - that the inexorable fall of rail was capable of being reversed - may well have registered a subconscious victory in places where the thought had not occurred before.

British Rail was emerging from a long period of dormancy. Its dynamic Chairman, Sir Peter Parker, had presence, personality, and a Pied Piper capacity for leading politicians by the nose. His crusading reign was followed by a period of retrenchment. Sectorisation placed the railway network on a sounder financial footing than it had enjoyed for generations. No one talked of closures any more, but of openings; stations initially, then whole lines. Local authorities were wooed and won over. Regional budgets were better spent wisely and accountably on rail improvements than frittered away on road schemes which often backfired by creating more traffic.

Individually, I remain to be convinced that privatisation was not conceived politically as a machiavellian means of derailing the railway's newly acquired head of steam, and I can only assume that those behind the blueprint badly miscalculated the powerful synergies it would unleash. As a model it may have been far from perfect, and will yet require revision to achieve a durable mould. But it introduced fresh blood to the railways and brought vision, optimism and a can-do culture where previously cynicism, pessimism and a couldn't-care-less attitude had held sway.

In 1990 the Norfolk Rail Policy Group was formed, a County Council initiative to enhance the region's railway network both for passengers and freight. Norfolk's burgeoning preserved lines were supported as well, amidst a growing recognition that rail development could deliver environmental benefits and improved quality of life for residents and visitors alike.

The concept of the Community Rail Partnership was a welcome by-product of privatisation. It focused new life into lines marginalised by decades of underfunding and disinterested management. Launched in 1996, the Bittern Line CRP was one of the first of its kind, and it is hardly coincidental that it has overseen 150% passenger growth on the Norwich - Sheringham route during the period of its existence. CRP's consist of interested parties (or 'stakeholders' in the jargon) such as local authorities, businesses, tourist groups and rail industry bodies. Four years after the Bittern Line CRP was formed the Wherry Lines launched their own partnership, by which time a successful and increasingly influential Association of Community Rail Partnerships had been founded under the acronym ACoRP.

This fresh focus on rural railways has gained government recognition, and new strategies are being developed to liberate the most fragile parts of the railway network from dogmatic engineering, marketing and costing practices more appropriate to suburban and inter city operations. In simpler terms, realisation has come (not entirely before time) that branch line railways can be operated and maintained on a fraction of the budget associated with busier routes without compromising reliability or safety issues. In some respects, privately preserved lines - such as the North Norfolk and Bure Valley railways featured in this guide - have pioneered these fresh approaches, reflecting less hidebound mind-sets together with an

Ole Kroczek

admirable awareness that inherently scenic rural railways can attract custom in their own right.

Scenery - its celebration and interpretation - naturally lies central to the scheme of things as far as this publication is concerned, and the routes featured within belie the Cowardesque misconception that all of Norfolk is 'flat, very flat'. The Fens, the Brecks, the Broads, the marshes, the North Norfolk coast constitute an infinite variety of landscapes accessible by rail and ripe for exploration. Ramblers, cyclists, bird-watchers, beer drinkers, bell-ringers, botanists and boaters represent merely the tip of an iceberg of enthusiasms likely to draw maximum enjoyment from journeying over the area covered by train. Fresh rolling stock offering improved views and enhanced seating arrangements and increased cycle space is being introduced on the Bittern and Wherry routes. One of these Class 156 units will wear a special Bittern & Wherry CRP livery to both advertise and celebrate the progress that these routes have made in recent years. In similar vein, the Brecks and Fen lines boast service levels and comfortable modern rolling stock calculated to woo even the most ardent motorists out of their cars. Whilst those ingrained with nostalgia for railway travel in the past are amply served by the North Norfolk, Bure Valley and emerging Mid-Norfolk lines.

Were you embarking on a romantic holiday in the district now I think you could safely go car-less, secure in the knowledge that by means of rail and bus and boat and bike hire, few corners of Norfolk's delectable landscapes would be denied you and the partner of your choice. In essence the whole railway network is enjoying a honeymoon of fresh partnerships and new allegiances, and I have a sneaking suspicion that time will ratify them all as marriages made in heaven.

Michael Pearson

The
BRECKS
Line

8

TWO Cambridge undergraduates, stumbling from the milk train after a night on London's tiles, commence the long walk back to college. 'I wish the station was nearer the town centre', remarks one balefully. Marginally the clearer headed, his boon companion rejoins: 'Yes, but I expect they thought it best to put it beside the railway line.'

As with Oxford, the University authorities of Cambridge kept the railway at arms length. Reputedly, seventeen sites were considered, and subsequently rejected, before a location agreeable to all parties was selected on the eastern edge of town. But if there were a Varsity Cup for railway station architecture, Cambridge would win hands down, Francis Thompson's colonnaded frontage far outshining the nondescript exterior which represented the Great Western Railway at Oxford until recent times. In the event, despite the hostility of town and gown, eight lines made their way into Cambridge from all corners of the compass. Only half of these remain, a melancholy average shared with Oxford.

Passing through the station's imposing facade - upon which the arms of Cambridge colleges are reconcilably displayed - the most striking feature confronting newcomers is the long, single-faced platform which caters for both up and down trains, a peculiar (though, at the dawn of railways, commonplace) arrangement made practical by the provision of a 'scissors crossing' half way along. Paired bays at either end provide accommodation for local services starting and terminating at Cambridge.

Officially unburdened, but leant identity by virtue of an hourly service provided by 'one' Anglia, the *Brecks Line* is a modern railway success story, ample evidence that clock-face operations between provincial centres can encourage large numbers to leave their cars behind. Departing from one or other of the north-facing bays, close by which you can enjoy pre-journey refreshments in a coffee bar adorned with archive railway images, Norwich bound trains snake over pointwork shared with services to King's Lyon, Peterborough and the Midlands.

Of three branches which left the main line north of Cambridge, only one survives. The Cambridge to Ipswich route remains a useful link through the middle of East Anglia, provided nowadays with an excellent hourly service by 'one' Anglia. The Mildenhall branch left the main line at Barnwell Junction. The line featured a sequence of seductive station

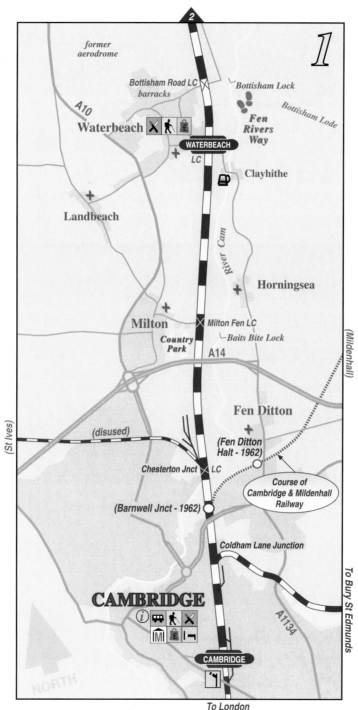

names like Quy, Bottisham & Lode, Swaffham Prior, Isleham, and Worlington Golf Links Halt, but beguiling proper nouns could not prevent it being closed in 1962. Theoretically, it might have carried thousands of airforce personnel based at Mildenhall into Cambridge on a bender, but the line's timetable was based on Cambridge and there was no way of getting into Cambridge early of an evening, and no way of getting back. Despite the introduction of railbuses towards the end, most local passengers from villages along the line found the rubber-tyred variety of bus more convenient. It would deliver them to the centre of Cambridge, not a mile down the road like the railway. In the Fifties, enthusiasts (not least the Cambridge University Railway Club) prized the Mildenhall branch for its use of veteran Great Eastern Railway E4 2-4-0s.

Another casualty has been the line running north-westwards to St Ives and beyond. St Ives lost its passenger trains comparatively recently in 1970 and there has long been a campaign to have them reintroduced, for the trackwork, albeit rusty and overgrown, remains in place. A counter-lobby prefers to see the route reconstituted as a guided bus-way, referred to by railway-inclined wits as a *mis*-guided bus-way. Up until 1959 trains used the St Ives line to reach Kettering via Huntingdon. In pre-grouping days this brought crimson-lake coloured Midland Railway trains into Cambridge.

Crossing the River Cam, on a bridge which traditionally marks the finish line of The Bumps rowing competitions, the Ely line finally escapes from the built up clutches of Cambridge, passes under the A14, and enters the definitive Fenland landscape. The lane which crosses the line at Milton Crossing runs down to Baits Bike Lock whose guillotine head gate may be glimpsed from the train. Beyond Milton the Cam comes close to the line. On the approach to Waterbeach there are remains of the Roman's Car Dyke to the west of the line. It ran from Cambridge to Lincoln, and by this means they transported East Anglian grain to the North two millennia ago. WATERBEACH provides transport facilities for a much expanded village with barracks on its northern outskirts. The aerodrome opened in 1941 and was associated from the outset with the not entirely reliable Stirling bomber. RAF Waterbeach survived into the Cold War, finally ceasing operations in 1963.

LONG miles of level track, beeline straight in their trajectory, do not necessarily make for a dull ride. The Fens stretch away from the carriage window like a modern work of art, requiring thought and interpretation to do them justice, more Mondrian than Constable. Black-soiled fields divided, not by hedges, but by drains, stretch away to the raised banks of the River Cam.

The Cam is navigable from its confluence with the Great Ouse at Pope's Corner for fourteen miles upstream to Cambridge. It is a fascinating river to navigate, but if you haven't a boat handy you can make use of the Fen Rivers Way to walk its banks, a fine day's tramp between Cambridge and Ely with the promise of refreshment at the Five Miles or Fish & Duck inns. The Five Miles is located on the site of a much older establishment known as the Five Miles From Anywhere - No Hurry, a riverside hostelry frequented by Fen lightermen and Cambridge undergraduates. Odd quaffing partners, one would imagine, but the latter group famously formed a drinking and debating club at the inn known as the Upware Republic!

Burwell Lode, which leaves the Cam at Upware, is also navigable, together with its side arms to Wicken and Reach. Wicken Fen is a remarkably preserved example of fenland as it appeared before being drained - 99.9% of former fenland environment is now under arable cultivation. This primordial landscape was saved by the National Trust as long ago as 1899, making it Britain's oldest nature reserve. Paradoxically water has now to be pumped *up* to Wicken Fen to give it the appearance of a wetland, the surrounding farmlands having shrunk and fallen below sea level. Like the members of a preserved railway society, those who care now for Wicken Fen have their work cut out to ensure that time stands still.

Similar efforts to preserve a piece of the past are also taking place to the west of the railway at the Farmland Museum & Denny Abbey. The abbey dates from the 12th century and over its history has been variously occupied by Benedictine monks, the Knights Templars and an order of Franciscan nuns known as the 'Poor Clares'. The Farmland Museum celebrates Cambridgeshire's rural heritage.

Prominent on the skyline to the west stands a tall chimney. This belongs to Stretham Old Engine, a pump house typical of the steam technology which replaced Fenland's windmills in Victorian times. The Boulton & Watt rotative beam engine at Stretham earned its living from 1831 to 1925, though it

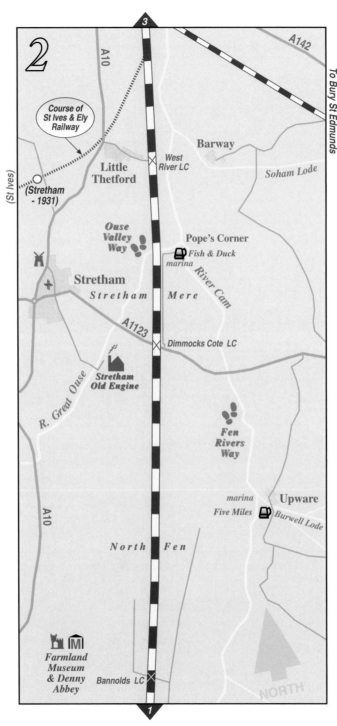

remained on standby until 1941, just in case the diesel engine which replaced it contracted a fault or needed a helping hand. Now both engines are preserved in the imposing buildings which housed them overlooking the Great Ouse. Ironically, the steam and diesel pumping machinery of The Fens was too efficient for its own good. The more water they pumped out of the neighbouring farmlands, the faster those farmlands shrank. Not before modern electric pumps were installed was some sort of equilibrium established.

The railway spans the Great Ouse close to its meeting place with the Cam at Pope's Corner. You can see patrons of the Fish & Duck bumping down a track alongside the line to quench their thirst. The Great Ouse rises near Brackley in Northamptonshire and reaches The Wash a hundred and sixty-five miles later. It is navigable from Bedford onwards, and in summer months you will often see cabin cruisers or narrow boats on the approaches to the railway bridge, and boating as an activity is likely to become more popular on these waters if the projected canal between Milton Keynes and Bedford comes to fruition.

Soham Lode joins the Great Ouse opposite Little Thetford, which was originally the site of a ford on the River Cam before the Dukes of Bedford hired Dutch engineers to redirect the region's river networks in the 17th century. Nowadays the town of Soham evokes dismal associations for reasons unconnected with railways, but on 2nd June, 1944 it was the scene of an act of considerable bravery on the part of a footplate crew of an ammunition train. Noticing that the first wagon of the train had caught fire, driver Benjamin Gimbert and fireman James Nightall uncoupled it from the remainder of the train and attempted to haul it out into open country. Despite their bravery the wagon exploded, killing the fireman and severely injuring the driver. But, in separating the burning wagon and its munitions from the rest of the train, Gimbert and Nightall had saved Soham from a devastating explosion. Soham station closed in 1965, but the line between Newmarket and Ely remains open and relatively busy.

In contrast, the branch line between Ely and St Ives lost its passenger trains as long ago as 1931. It might not have enjoyed over much success as a passenger line, but in the days before road lorries became so ubiquitous, it played a vital part in the distribution of Fenland farm produce, remaining open for goods until 1964.

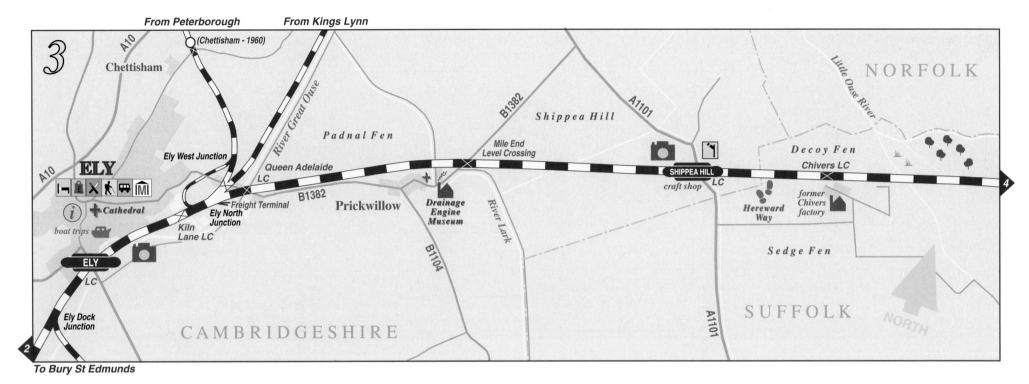

ELY vies with Durham in the 'Best View of a Cathedral from a Train' competition: Truro, Worcester and York mere runners up. One can only suppose the 19th century bishops felt sacrosanct on their hilltop from the vulgarity of the railway. In all too many other locations the railway was made to hide itself from view, as one would hide the servants quarters from the gaze of visiting gentry.

Neither could the church prevent Ely from becoming a busy junction. Geographically there was no obvious alternative. The wonder is that the town did not grow commercially and industrially, so possibly the ecclesiastical authorities did have some influence; or perhaps it was just a matter of there being too little firm ground surrounding what, after all, had originally been the Isle of Ely. For their part the railway builders provided Ely with a handsome, if austere, station. A small, but curious, point concerns the canopy on the down platform which doesn't lean over as far as the platform edge. This was not cheese-paring on the builders' account! Originally there were three running lines between the down and up platforms. When the line to King's

Lynn was electrified one was removed and the platform, but not the canopy, extended outwards.

Nevertheless, Ely remains an attractive station on which to saunter between connections, or simply somewhere to sit at patio tables thoughtfully provided by the coffee bar and watch the Fenland world go by. Hamilton Ellis joked that to Oxford Undergraduates the architecture of Ely station comically resembled nothing so much as Oxford University's Queen's College. His earliest memory of the Great Eastern Railway, as evoked in his book *The Beauty of Old Trains* (George Allen & Unwin, 1952) was of a Claud Hamilton 'rushing across the Fens under a stormy sky, with Ely Cathedral riding in the distance like a great ship'.

The cathedral's ship-like analogy is not original to Hamilton Ellis. Nor is it the only visual marine pun in the neighbourhood. As the train pulls out of Ely you could be forgiven for thinking that you had already reached the coast as a busy marina comes into view, stuffed to the gills with cabin cruisers and narrow boats. These are the boatyards of the Great Ouse, known as the Island of Babylon. Nowadays

it is all part of the leisure industry, but once the boatbuilders were more concerned with trade. There were maltings and timber wharves and, in the early days of the railway, a transhipment dock where coal could be transferred from railways wagons into Fenland lighters for onward transport to villages remote from the railway. Another fluvial activity concerned the extraction of clay, colloquially known as gault, from riverside pits for use as a lining in the maintenance of the riverbanks. Nowadays the pits have been flooded and find use with Ely Sailing Club.

Skirting the flooded clay workings, the Ely West Curve makes its isolated way through reedbeds and marshy ground to effect a passage for trains wishing to avoid the time-consuming complications of reversal at Ely station. Boxing the compass as it does, it was never an easy bit of railway to describe, and has also been confusingly referred to as the South and North curve on occasion. No scheduled passenger trains use this by-pass now, but two or three goods trains do, notably the sand trains travelling from King's Lynn and Yorkshire and empty stone trains between Norwich and

Mountsorrel near Loughborough. Oddly, though the curve is bi-directionally signalled, it is only currently passed for operation in the March direction.

Passing Potter's reassuringly busy rail freight terminal the train for Norwich leaves the March and King's Lynn lines at Ely North Junction and heads in a north-easterly direction across the Great Ouse at Queen Adelaide. This man-made section of the river dates from the 19th century and is known as Sandall's Cut.

Leaving Ely and civilisation astern feels like abandoning home for the first time. Intimidated by the vast, limitless fens, your eye searches for something homely to focus on, however insignificant. These acres of arable crops must surely have been sewn by human hand, or at least a mechanical version of the same, but it is difficult to be entirely convinced. Old maps reveal that there was a railway siding on Padnal Fen, presumably it was employed for the transport of vegetables before the ubiquitous lorry took over.

Pylons are of little reassurance, but the village of Prickwillow is; surprisingly never afforded the luxury of a railway station. Here the line crosses the River Lark, a tributary of the Great Ouse, navigable upstream as far as Isleham, though its source lies much further to the south, beyond Bury St Edmunds in deepest Suffolk. Until 1827 the Ouse flowed from Ely to Littleport via Prickwillow. A fascinating museum devoted to the history of Fenland drainage is located in the village and features a marvellous array of pumping machinery, an arcane subject of enthusiasm which makes trainspotting almost mainstream. A tablet, dated 1842, on display outside the museum pays homage to 'steam, mighty steam' and its 'unlimited, untiring power'! So damp were things in Prickwillow, however, that the church had to be built on piles and the dead had to be buried in Ely on account of the water table being too high.

Progress has been hit and miss along this line. At Mile End the level crossing has been automated and the signal box demolished. In contrast, at SHIPPEA HILL, the box survives and crossing gates are traditionally built of timber. A drove road approaches this remote station from the south-west, lined with trees in a manner reminiscent of France. When the line was opened this wayside halt was resonantly known as Mildenhall Drove & Burnt Fen. It would be good to have the original nameboard in one's collection of railwayana. Few trains deign to call here now - presumably to avoid the Parliamentary complications of complete closure. Incidentally, Burnt Fen is said to derive its incinerated name from Hereward the Wake's scorched earth policy.

But Shippea Hill - which gets its unlikely suffix from a nearby outcrop of clay where prehistoric remains were unearthed - was once significantly busier and even ran to a 'Railway Tavern' - now an enterprising craft shop. There were public sidings here, together with characteristic employee housing, but also a private line into the premises of Chivers, the jam and jelly manufacturers, who had a factory here and fruit orchards alongside the railway. The premises are now used by a manufacturer of irrigation products, but a level crossing steadfastly recalls Chivers name as the line crosses from Cambridgeshire into Suffolk. Up passenger trains were given special dispensation to stop here and collect fruit-filled wagons from the works.

Shippea Hill

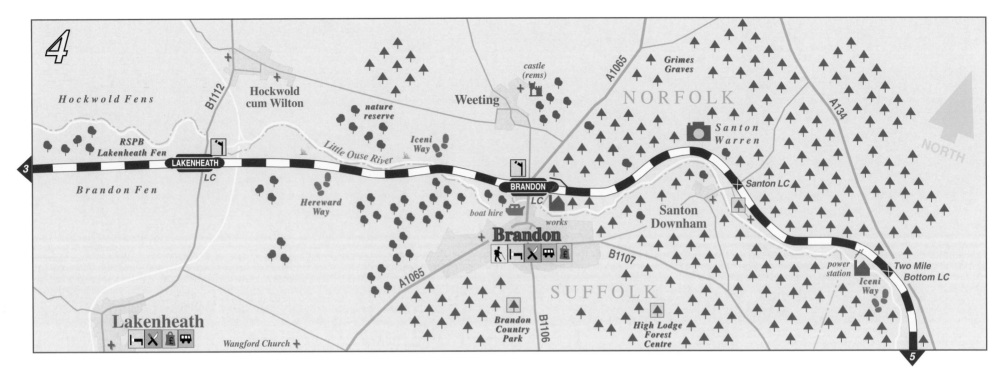

POPLAR plantations provide some welcome relief to the horizontal landscape. Many of these trees have already been felled to make matchsticks, but those which survive provide a habitat for the rare Golden Oriole.

Lengthy queues of traffic are apt to build up at the numerous level crossings on this line. Those at LAKEN-HEATH are likely to consist of many left-hand drive vehicles driven by American servicemen stationed at the important air base south and east of the town. RAF Mildenhall is also nearby. In the past military activity brought a good deal of traffic to the railway. The Booking Clerk at Lakenheath was under instructions from headquarters to accept American currency for ticket purchases. Nowadays the service is as sparse as Shippea Hill and the station unmanned. The signalman works the timber crossing gates, traffic signals aiding him in the interruption of traffic on the busy B1112. Its back broken, an ancient clerestory coach disintegrates in lineside undergrowth.

East of Lakenheath the line crosses a water channel which conveys excess waters from Denver Sluice to Essex, but it is the Little Ouse, paralleling the railway and forming the county boundary between Suffolk and Norfolk, which captures your attention, in flirtatious frame of mind before it passes beneath you and disappears in search of the fleshpots of Brandon. Currently navigable thus far, a project has been launched to consider the possibility of allowing boats to reach Thetford again, a feat not possible since navigation weirs along the upper reaches of the river fell into disrepair prior to the First World War.

BRANDON is better served than the previous two stations on the line. Its signal box dates from LNER days when powered points were introduced in the vicinity. Unusually, the frame is on the back wall. Brandon has been designated a 'Gateway Station' by the Countryside Agency as part of their initiative to revitalise Market Towns. Certainly it could do with a magic wand to rekindle the innate yet decidedly latent appeal of its brick and flint construction. And it deserves a better environment, for historically this was the end-on junction of the Eastern Counties and Norfolk & Brandon (or Norfolk) railway companies when the line was opened in 1845. One of the first excursions was to Norwich for a public hanging. Equally dolefully the station is now overlooked by a breeze-block works, whilst all which remains of a once sizeable and busy goods yard is a single siding, used occasionally for stone and timber traffics.

A remarkable change comes over the landscape east of Brandon. The Fens are but a memory, welcome to the open heaths and forestry plantations of Breckland. But don't imagine that all these conifers are indigenous. The regimented plantations are the work of the Forestry Commission from the 1920s onwards, the beautiful and iconic belts of arthritically twisted Scots Pine somewhat earlier, deliberately planted as wind breaks to prevent, or at least lessen, the erosion of valuable topsoil. The term 'Brecks' can be defined as ground temporarily cultivated. The sandy and chalky soils of this region could not sustain crops for an unlimited amount of time, its most productive activities were flint-knapping and rabbit-warrening.

Flint occurs naturally in bands of chalk, and the activity of flint-knapping goes back to the prehistoric need for simple tools. As man grew more sophisticated he saw flint's potential for weaponry. Rather than on the playing fields of Eton, it has been said that the Battle of Waterloo was won in the flint-knapperies of Brandon. Nowadays, more peacefully, local flint is used as a decorative material in buildings.

Breckland's soft, sandy soils were ideal for the creation of artificial burrows in medieval times. Rabbit meat was as big a business hereabouts in those days as poultry farming is now, and the 'battery' farming methods employed equally restrictive. Though over the years, as rabbits 'escaped' and multiplied (as only rabbits can) their grazing habits quickened erosion. The rabbits were not only valued for their meat, their pelts were used for clothing. As an industry warrening survived into the early years of the 20th century. Ironically, as the forest developed, attempts were made to eradicate the diminishing numbers of rabbits which remained in the wild and were now regarded as pests, myxomatosis being deliberately introduced.

The railway responds to the change in landscape. Gradients are encountered for virtually the first time since Ely, as the line follows the valley of the Little Ouse, and there are curves as well, though actually the original intention was for the line to make more or less directly for Attleborough with a branch being built to serve Thetford. After the emptiness of the fens, it is fun to journey through the forest. While steam remained the prime form of motive power on this line, up until the early 1960s, special care was taken to prevent lineside fires, in case they should spread and set the forest ablaze. Perversely, the threat of fire was at its greatest during the summer months when the line was carrying additional passenger services to and from the Norfolk coast. On one occasion no less than ninety lineside fires were set ablaze in the course of a day by passing trains.

In earlier times, sandstorms were not uncommon. In 1668 the village of Santon Downham was effectively buried in sand. Nestling in the woods, neighbouring Santon's tiny church is pastorally redundant. Richard Kendal, a rector here during the Civil War, was ejected by the Parliamentarians for 'swearing, haunting inns, being distempered by liquor, keeping malignant company, and for saying that the Puritans were hypocrites'. He was reinstated when the monarchy was restored! Hereabouts Jacob sheep are to be seen grazing by the lineside. These felled areas of forest provide a conducive habitat for rare birds, notably the Stone Curlew, Woodlark and Nightjar.

On the banks of the Little Ouse, at Two Mile Bottom, Fisons had a rail and river-served fertilizer factory. Nowadays the site plays host to an unusual power station which derives its fuel from chicken litter brought in by lorry from the numerous poultry farms in the area. The plant generates enough electricity to provide power for over sixty-thousand households, whilst the waste ash, rich in potash and phosphate, is marketed as an environmentally friendly fertilizer.

Something else has altered since Brandon, a subtlety you can't quite put your finger on until it hits you in the face. Telegraph poles!

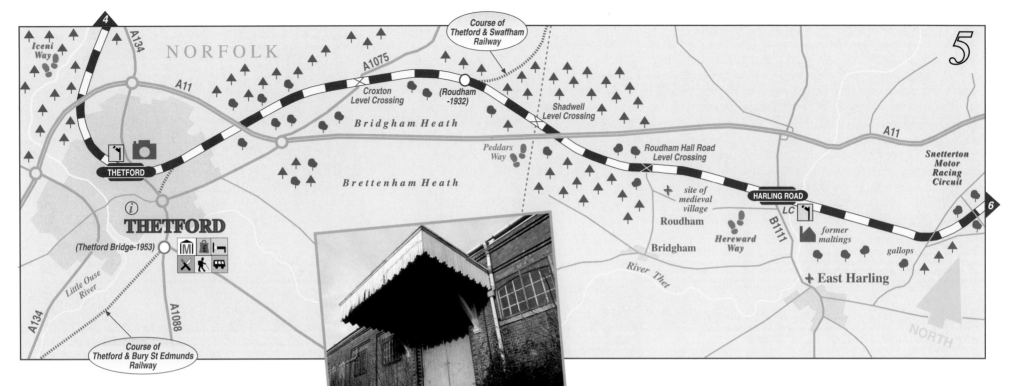

Map labels:

4 5

NORFOLK

Iceni Way

A134

A11

A1075

Course of Thetford & Swaffham Railway

Croxton Level Crossing

(Roudham -1932)

Shadwell Level Crossing

Bridgham Heath

Peddars Way

Brettenham Heath

THETFORD

ⓘ THETFORD

(Thetford Bridge-1953)

Little Ouse River

A134

A1088

Course of Thetford & Bury St Edmunds Railway

Roudham Hall Road Level Crossing

A11

Snetterton Motor Racing Circuit

✝ site of medieval village

Roudham

HARLING ROAD

LC

B1111

Hereward Way

former maltings

gallops

Bridgham

River Thet

✝ East Harling

NORTH

6

YES, telegraph poles! An extremely rare survival of a once commonplace facet of the railway scene. One can only think of the Aberdeen to Inverness line as featuring these lines of communication between signal boxes now, virtually all other routes still reliant on mechanical signalling having buried their telegraph wires in lineside conduits long ago. That they have survived between Brandon and Wymondham is purely - but happily as far as traditionalists are concerned - due to a lack of investment, but their days are undoubtedly numbered. After all, many of the telegraph posts themselves are thought to date from the installation of the telegraph system on this line in the early days of the Boer War. Some are said to be supported by the wires these days rather than the other way round! But it will be sad to see such a time-honoured aspect of the railway environment disappear altogether. Signallers will tell you that the telegraph wires have a life of their own, being prone to cross currents on damp days. One tale goes that the signalman at Somerleyton (Map 20) once overhead a conversation emanating from the box at Spooner Row in such conditions.

Climbing under the A11 by-pass the railway emerges from the forest and skirts an industrial zone on its way into THETFORD. By virtue of its population - boosted by overspill schemes - this is the most important stop between Ely and Norwich. Handsome though it undoubtedly is, however, the station seems oddly claustrophobic. You need to alight to do the architecture justice, to appreciate the subtle intricacies of the canopy valances and cast-iron supports boasting the delightful detail of spoked wheels. On the up, westbound platform there are not one, but two station buildings, the 1845 original with its pointed Jacobean gables having been bolstered, forty years later, by a less glamorous addition as business boomed. Now, only the newer, redbrick building remains in use, the only staffed station between Ely and Norwich.

Thetford became a railway crossroads. There were branch lines southwards to Bury St Edmunds and north to Swaffham. These lines had been promoted as part of an ambitious scheme for a line to run through the centre of East Anglia between Bury St Edmunds and King's Lynn. The route was to be grandiloquently known as the Midland, Eastern & Great Northern Junction Railway. Amongst its backers was Edward Greene, the Bury brewer. The Railway Mania spawned numerous such schemes. Many were never built at all, others were built but never achieved anything beyond branch line status. An east curve at Thetford, long ago buried under housing schemes, was abandoned as early as 1880, and with it went all hope of through running, a lost facility which had cause to be regretted during the Second World War when large numbers of ammunition trains and troop trains used the lines. Passenger services ceased running from Bury St Edmunds in 1953, the Swaffham line (nicknamed the 'Crab & Winkle') lasted another eleven years. Goods survived until 1960 on the Bury line, nuclear bombs being carried to a base at Barnham! Thetford Bridge station was for a while used as a Youth Hostel.

You pull out of Thetford past allotments and housing in a north-easterly direction, passing once again beneath the A11 and re-entering a Breckland landscape. Telegraph poles, briefly

16

absent, are welcomed back like old friends, the rise and fall of the wires between poles becoming somewhat hypnotic, like the conversational gambits of one's nearest and dearest.

Pig farms proliferate as the train approaches ROUDHAM JUNCTION, one of those self-contained railway communities which sprang up where lines diverged remote of any larger settlement. Deep in the woods now, it reminds you of Pilmoor on the East Coast Main Line between York and Thirsk. Similarly there are old employees cottages still occupied by new generations of non-railwaymen, and just the ghosts of connecting trains. A platelayers hut provides a strange memorial to lost activity. Officially, the last train called in 1932 - unofficially, stops continued to be made so that the railwaymen's wives could go shopping in Thetford.

Shadwell Crossing ushers Peddars Way over the line. This is thought to date from the Roman period and Boudica's revolt circa AD61. Most probably it was constructed to subjugate the Iceni. So it seems most ironic that its modern day status is that of a long distance path, used, not by security-conscious Legionnaires but mild-mannered ramblers. It runs from Knettishall Heath Country Park to the east of Thetford to Holme-next-the-Sea on the North Norfolk Coast where it links up with the Norfolk Coast Path which you will meet again in this book on the *Bittern Line*. En route it crosses land given over to military manoeuvres, and so any soldiery encountered may not merely be those of Roman spirits. The Hereward Way also crosses the line at Shadwell. This is a 110 mile long distance path stretching from East Harling to Rutland via Brandon, Ely and Peterborough. Part of it follows Harling Drove, a herding trail predating even the Romans.

Roudham is a shrunken medieval village, blighted by the Black Death in 1349. Its parish church, St Andrew's, can be seen to the south of the line as the train proceeds to

Harling Road, a ruin since 1736 when a workman absent-mindedly set light to the thatched roof when knocking out the ashes from his pipe. There are 18th century drainage ditches alongside the railway, previously there was a large mere. HARLING ROAD is one of the Breckland Line's sparsely-served halts, but at least a pair of morning eastbound stoppers give walkers the opportunity of an early start to the Hereward Way. There was a sizeable granary here linked to the railway. Nissen huts are left over from World War II when there was a stores depot here. The line crosses the River Thet, a tributary of the Little Ouse, just east of the station. The Rector at West Harling between 1899 and 1915, Charles Hugh Richardson Harper, was also the *Daily Telegraph's* bee-keeping correspondent, and later in life wrote a travel book entitled *The Motorist's Ceylon*! When he stepped off the train at Harling Road to take up his incumbency - following a three hour journey from Liverpool Street - he was met by a four-wheeled dog cart drawn by a silver-grey horse driven by the local squire. Alight here today and you'll be met by - birdsong and not a lot else!

The Breckland landscape begins to give way to a more tame, agricultural countryside. You encounter yet another pig farm. On jointed track the train appears to 'gallop' simultaneously with the appearance of racing horse gallops in the neighbouring fields. You catch a glimpse of the motor racing circuit at Snetterton, built on the site of an old wartime aerodrome, before brackeny cuttings engulf you. Snetterton was home to the 96th Bomb Group, one of the most illustrious units of the Eighth Air Force, though also one of the most affected by casualties. *Memphis Belle*, a B17 bomber plane made famous by two feature films, flew from here.

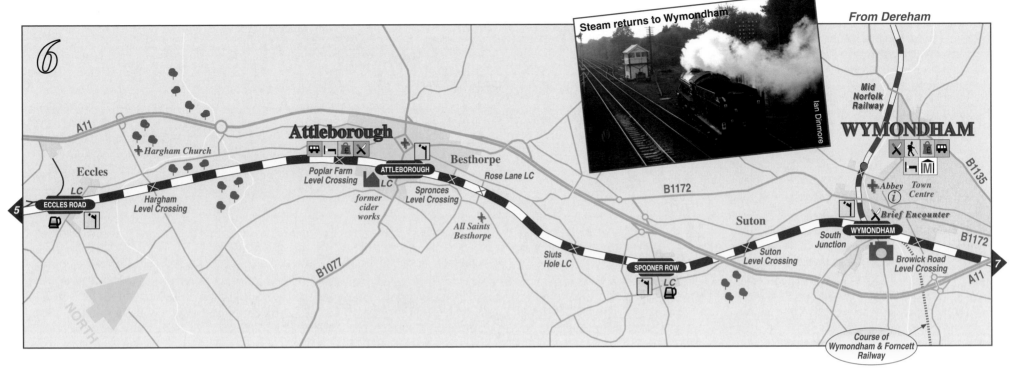

Steam returns to Wymondham

From Dereham

Attleborough

Eccles
Hargham Church
A11

ECCLES ROAD

Hargham
Level Crossing

Poplar Farm
Level Crossing

*former
cider
works*

Besthorpe

Rose Lane LC

Spronces
Level Crossing

*All Saints
Besthorpe*

Sluts
Hole LC

SPOONER ROW

B1077

Suton
Level Crossing

Suton

South
Junction

WYMONDHAM

Brief Encounter

*Browick Road
Level Crossing*

A11

B1172

B1172

WYMONDHAM

*Mid
Norfolk
Railway*

B1135

Abbey   Town
Centre

*Course of
Wymondham & Forncett
Railway*

Ian Dinmore

NORTH

JOINTED track (some of which, amazingly, dates back to the 1920s) telegraph poles, hand operated level crossings: solely the train seems of this century! A rusty branch line curves away to the north. It is not as old as it looks, having been laid as recently as 1985 to serve a grain silo. Regrettably it was out of use within five years, a victim of British Rail's intransigent attitude to freight customers, the premise being that goods trains were operated to suit the railway's timetable rather than the customer's requirements. Mothballed now, it was briefly used again a couple of years back for the carriage of materials associated with improvements to the A11.

ECCLES ROAD 'serves' a scattering of small heathland settlements: Quidenham, Wilby, Hargam and Snetterton; the inverted commas emphasise the paucity of the timetable. In Quidenham Church there's a stained glass memorial to the American air crews of Snetterton Heath. At Wilby there was a cricket team during Victoria's reign consisting of eleven brothers. Hargam's ruined church is just visible, through winter's bare branches, to the north of the railway. Poplar Farm level crossing is hand worked by a crossing keeper

resident in a refurbished plate-layers hut, the original flint-built keeper's house having been sold into private ownership.

Through dappled birch plantations the line runs to ATTLEBOROUGH, passing flint-built crossing-keepers cottages en route. Attleborough's staggered platforms are enhanced in summertime with floral displays tended by the signalmen. The large brick built station building on the down side is occupied by a veterinary practice and a pet behavioural centre! A tablet above the old entrance to the booking hall commemorates the 452 Bomb Group who flew B17s out of Deopham Green. Across the tracks stands a big, ivy-clad, brick-built goods shed with Gothic windows.

Attleborough was long known as a centre for turkeys and cider. Sadly, Gaymers lineside cider works closed in 1995, production of the brand being transferred to Bristol. They must have provided a good deal of traffic for the railway in their time. Gaymers moved here in 1896 from Banham. An old photograph in the Middleton Press's nostalgic *Ely to Norwich* album (ISBN 1 901706 90 7) shows row upon row of cider barrels stacked by the company's private sidings. Since Gaymers departure the works has become a poultry

processing plant. The train climbs out of Attleborough at 1 in 467, encountering a number of level crossings in the process. South of Rose Lane crossing, Besthorpe's parish church of All Saints stands remote from its village. A family vault contained the coffin of Viscount Kilmorey, interred here in 1668 at the age of thirteen. The coffin was opened in 1877 and found to contain not bones, but books! To the south lay Old Buckenham aerodrome, an American base during World War Two. James Stewart, the Hollywood actor, was stationed here in 1944.

The next level crossing goes by the intriguing name of Sluts Hole. It is followed, alliteratively, by SPOONER ROW; how you begin to wish that Larkin or Betjeman had known this line and penned some appropriately plangent verse in its honour. Swallows nest in the eaves of Spooner Row's signal box. Railway cottages overlook the down platform. The station building on the up platform has been demolished.

As the train passes beneath the A11, you catch sight of Wymondham Abbey to the north, before a down loop, used for splitting aggregates trains bound for Trowse, announces Wymondham South Junction. This marks the egress of the Dereham line which lost its passenger services in 1969, but which is now part of the Mid Norfolk Railway preserved line. Unfortunately, as yet, MNR trains are denied access to the main line station, prospective through travellers facing a twenty minute walk to their terminus known as Wymondham Abbey, though NENTA tour trains do travel over the link, along with other operators rolling stock using the MNR for training purposes and trials.

The Dereham line carried services to both King's Lynn via Swaffham and Wells-next-the-Sea via Fakenham, withdrawn beyond Dereham in 1968 and 1964 respectively. When diesel multiple units were introduced on the Wells line the transport of locally caught cockles played havoc with the underfloor engines on account of the juices leaking through to the machinery. Another regular traffic was in pilgrims destined for the shrine at Walsingham. It is a great shame that neither of these useful lines survived, for along with the demise of the Hunstanton line, North-west Norfolk became a railway desert. Currently preserved steam and diesel trains operate between Wymondham Abbey and Dereham, but the MNR have plans to extend these eleven miles northwards by another six to County School. As an independent line it has terrific potential.

A signal box overlooks the junction. Once there was a turntable here as well, for turning branch line engines. The base of a former water tower is another indication of working practices now forgotten. WYMONDHAM station was an award winner in the 2004 Anglia in Bloom competition, a scene of total transformation from the all but derelict days of twenty years ago when the station more resembled Brandon (Map 4) now. Wymondham's rescue hinged on a chance visit by piano dealer and businessman, David Turner. In 1987, as guest of a British Rail inspection tour, he was appalled to see what state the station he had known and loved as a child had been reduced to. Within two years, David dynamically restored the station building, initially making use of it as a piano showroom, then subsequently adding a splendid refreshment room known, after the famous Trevor Howard/Celia Johnson film as the *Brief Encounter.* Whatever your planned itinerary, it is difficult to resist getting off the train to explore this beautifully restored station; wherever your gaze falls there is something to delight the eye; casting your mind back to Brandon you wonder why all stations don't

attract such imaginative care and devotion.

Built of flint and brick, the station has the air of a country parsonage. More chapel-like, the old goods shed stands at right angles to the running lines, a trait peculiar to the Norwich & Brandon Railway, access originally being via a wagon turntable. Business in the goods yard was brisk and continued to be so right up until the 1980s. A private siding ran into the premises of the Briton Brush Company, for many years one of the town's main employers. Inwards goods consisted of raw materials from as far afield as Africa and Mexico. Finished products were despatched by a daily train. Each year the company ran a seaside special for its workforce, the locomotive's smokebox graced by a headboard featuring their trademark windmill. Britons closed down in 1985 and a housing estate now occupies the site of the works. Nowadays Wymondham's best known establishments are the headquarters of the Norfolk County Constabulary, and the workshops of Lotus sports cars.

Long-vanished, Wymondham North Junction was the point at which a branch to Forncett on the Ipswich to Norwich line curved away to the south-east. Double track, it had opened in 1881 amidst high hopes of it developing as a through route to the North Norfolk Coast avoiding Norwich. But resorts such as Wells and Blakeney never developed sufficiently to warrant through expresses from Liverpool Street, and trains were of a desultory local character, albeit delightfully nicknamed the 'Swede and Swimmer'. Paradoxically the line came into its own during the Second World War just as regular services were abandoned. The Americans had a military hospital on the outskirts of Wymondham. Following the D-Day Landings eight hospital trains conveyed over two thousand wounded to this establishment where the benefits of penicillin were being researched and developed. In its twilight years the Forncett line was used for wagon storage pending scrapping. Rolling stock was gutted by fire before being broken up, but what price some of those vehicles now? The concept of railway preservation was in its infancy in those days and many then seemingly mundane but now irreplaceable items were destroyed by the infidels conspicuously lacking in David Turner's compassion.

SOME 150 feet above sea level, the Ely-Norwich line's summit is at Ketteringham, at which point the railway runs alongside the A11, drawing inevitable comparisons between transport modes. Thereafter, the railway heads downhill through the Yare Valley towards Norwich. Hethersett lost its station in the Sixties before it became a large dormitory village on the doorstep of Norwich. The buildings remain, a flash of flint and valenced canopy backed by a military oil dump, still ostensibly rail served. Leaving traditional signalling methods behind, you come under the control of a power signal box located as far away as Colchester.

In no time at all the line falls a hundred feet, finding itself in a landscape of watermeadows adjoining the Yare. A weatherboarded water mill comes into view at Keswick as the river is spanned in quick succession several times. The valley allows the line from Ely a level approach to Norwich. In contrast the line from Ipswich, completed in 1849, approaches the city at a much higher level, bridging the River Yare and your line by way of Lakenham Viaduct. A handsome structure of six arches, laying of the foundation stone on the 30th August, 1847, was followed confidently by a 'broaching of beer barrels', but such optimism was misplaced, and the structure took two frustrating years to complete, delaying the railway's entry from the south. Whilst the Ipswich line has always been regarded as the main route between Norwich and London, the alternative - by way of Ely and Cambridge - was provided with through services for many years. Surprisingly, the latter route is just ten miles longer.

Closely accompanied by the Yare, the railway curves round to join the Ipswich line at Trowse. The watermeadows preclude urban expansion, and the landscape is remarkably unaltered since Trowse was a favoured viewpoint for painters of the Norwich School, notably John Crome (1768-1821) and John Sell Cotman (1782-1842). They and their followers - including four of Crome's children and two of Cotman's - favoured realism and depicted an Arcadian, pre-industrial Norfolk in watercolours and oils. John Sell Cotman painted a watercolour of wherry sailing barges at Trowse Hythe in 1810, his son, John Joseph Cotman, painted Trowse Meadows in oils in 1860.

There is an inevitability, however, surrounding the onset of the city's built up periphery. Overlooked by County Hall, headquarters of the Bittern and Wherry Community Rail Partnerships, the lines meet at Trowse Lower Junction, merging

at the site of Trowse station. A riverside aggregates depot receives deliveries by rail from Mountsorrel near Loughborough. The only other commodity regularly to arrive in the city by rail is limestone destined for the sugar beet works at Cantley (Map 19) which completes its journey by road. This telling statistic is in stark contrast to the past when the vast majority of goods arriving or departing from Norwich went by river or rail. One of the city's most famous companies, Colmans the mustard makers, had riverside premises at Carrow served by a private branch from Trowse. Trowse was a name which struck horror into the hearts of those who loved steam, for this was the location of King's scrapyard where many fine locomotives met their destiny with the breaker's torch.

The track now singles to cross the River Wensum on a modern, single track swing-bridge put in place when the London line was electrified in 1986. Although commercial trade has ceased now on the river, a sufficient number of tall masted yachts and leisure craft continue to use the river necessitating movement of the bridge, for which there are six pre-bookable slots each day. As well as overseeing bridge movements, the signal box at Trowse uses computer-based signalling methods to control trains on the *Bittern Line*.

Railway fans will be straining to catch a glimpse of the occupants of Crown Point Depot whilst football fans will be on the look out for Carrow Road, Norwich Football Club's imposing modern stadium. Those with no enthusiasm for either will be making for the doors as the train pulls into one of provincial England's most impressive termini, now simply known as NORWICH, but once called Norwich Thorpe to distinguish it from the city's other termini: Norwich Victoria and Norwich City. Victoria lay at the end of the Eastern Union Railway's Ipswich line. It opened in 1849 but was soon playing second fiddle to Norwich Thorpe and closed to passengers during the First World War. Into the 1980s it saw use as a coal concentration depot. Norwich City, located on the north side of the city, belonged to the Midland & Great Northern Railway.

But Norwich Thorpe was born to be the city's enduring railway statement and it marches into the 21st century with its concourse playing host to a cluster of retail outlets at which to purchase all the seemingly essential paraphernalia of the modern railway journey. Gorge yourself by all means, but don't forget to admire the architecture before setting off to explore the Bittern and Wherry lines.

From Cromer, Yarmouth & Lowestoft

7

Wensum Junction
Crown Point Depot
Thorpe Jnct.
Swing Bridge Junction
Cathedral
NORWICH
Trowse Swing Br.
City Centre
Norwich City FC
aggregates depot
R. Wensum
(Trowse - 1939)
Castle
County Hall
Trowse Lower Junction
(City - 1959)
(Victoria - 1916)
R. Tas

NORWICH

£ ⚒ ✕ 🚶 🚌 Ⓜ

Lakenham Viaduct

A146

R. Yare
A140

watermill
Keswick

A47
Keswick LC
Intwood LC

B1172

oil depot
(Hethersett - 1966)
monument

Hethersett

Ketteringham

summit

A11

NORTH

6

Gazetteer

Attleborough
Map 6

Untypical of Norfolk, Attleborough is a small manufacturing town curiously bedevilled by road traffic, exacerbated by lengthy queues when the level crossing closes. Whatever virtues it may possess in the eyes of its natives, it is difficult to imagine it ever appealing to tourists in any great degree. Its cider-making past sounds more salubrious, and the annual Turkey Fair to which many of the birds were herded from distant parts of East Anglia on foot, their feet reinforced for the often epic journey by tar.

Brandon
Map 4

A town whose colourful past was concerned with flint-knapping and the fur trade, and now a good launch pad for exploring Thetford Forest and The Brecks. The flint knapping industry was at its zenith during the Napoleonic Wars, but ceased commercially in the 1970s. Once there were three fur factories in the town. When the rabbit fur had been processed, much of it went by rail to other parts of the country to be used by hat makers. Quite the best thing you can do on a summer's day is to make the short walk from the station to the river bridge where rowing boats are available for hire.

Accommodation
BRANDON HOUSE HOTEL - Bridge Street. Tel: 01842 810171 *www.brandonhouse.co.uk* Two star hotel within two hundred and fifty yards of the station and alongside the Little Ouse. Handsome former 18th century merchant's home.
RIVERSIDE LODGE - Bridge Street. Tel: 01842 811236. Bed & breakfast on the riverbank.

Eating & Drinking
CUOCO PAZZO - Bridge Street. Tel: 01842 811010. Italian/Maltese cooking in annex to the Great Eastern Hotel, a pub beside the railway station which also offers bed & breakfast.
COLLINS - High Street. Tel: 01842 811766. Fish & chip restaurant.
BRIDGE HOUSE - Bridge Street. Tea room with rowing boats for hire during the summer months - Tel: 01842 811236.
Several take-aways in the High Street within 5 minutes walk of the station.

Shopping
Market day on Thursdays. Co-op supermarket.

Things to Do
TOURIST INFORMATION - High Street. Tel: 01842 814955 *www.brecks.org*
HERITAGE CENTRE - George Street. Local history. Check with TIC for opening times. Starting point for a Town Trail which will introduce you to elements of Brandon's past.
BRANDON COUNTRY PARK - south of town centre on B1106. Tel: 01842 810185. Waymarked forest trails etc.
HIGH LODGE FOREST CENTRE - located 3 miles south-east of Brandon off the B1107. Forest leisure activities, bike hire, shop and

cafeteria. Tel: 01842 815434.
GRIMES GRAVES - located 4 miles north-east of Brandon off A1065. Don a hard hat and descend into Neolithic flint mines. Tel: 01842 810656.

Walking
Brandon station provides easy access to the Iceni Way (Thetford-Holme next the Sea) and Hereward Way (Harling-Rutland). The Little Ouse Path follows the river between Brandon and Thetford, a gentle 10 mile stroll through the forest with good train services at either end.

Boating
Rowing boat hire from Easter to October - Tel: 01842 811236.

Connections
TAXIS - Carter's. Tel: 01842 811430. Borders - Tel: 01842 814488.
CYCLE HIRE - Bike Art at High Lodge Forest Centre. Tel: 01842 810090.

Cambridge
Map 1

More serene than its academic counterpart four counties away to the west, Cambridge can be assessed self-indulgently from the open top deck of the tour buses which depart the railway station every quarter of an hour or so. Familiarity can be a more drawn out process; the fortunate, if transient, tenure of undergraduates to whom, paradoxically, it will mean more after it is all over.

Accommodation
SLEEPERZ HOTEL - Station Road. Tel: 01223 304050 *www.sleeperz.com* Stylish budget style en suite accommodation in a converted granary alongside the station.
GONVILLE HOTEL - Gonville Place. Tel: 01223 366611 *www.bw-gonvillehotel.co.uk* Best Western 3 Star hotel located between the railway station and the town centre.
ACCOMMODATION BOOKING SERVICE - Tel: 01223 457581 *www.visitcambridge.org*

Eating & Drinking
LE GROS FRANK - Hills Road. Tel: 01223 565560. Exceptional French restaurant less than 5 minutes walk from the station where Station Road gives way to Hills Road.
THE VARSITY RESTAURANT - St Andrews Street. Tel: 01223 356060. Spick and span restaurant established as long ago as 1954. About quarter of an hour's walk from the station on the way into the town centre.
THE COPPER KETTLE - King's Parade. Tel: 01223 365068. Old fashioned cafe/restaurant overlooking King's College.

Shopping
Useful branch of Marks & Spencer on the station for picnic making. Excellent market Monday to Saturday in the town centre.

Things to Do
TOURIST INFORMATION - Wheeler Street. Tel: 0906 5862526 *www.visitcambridge.org*
FITZWILLIAM MUSEUM - Trumpington Street. Tel: 01223 332900 *www.fitzmuseum.cam.ac.uk* World famous art gallery colloquially known as 'The Fitz'.

KING'S COLLEGE - King's Parade. Tel: 01223 331100 *www.kings.cam.ac.uk* Incomparable 15th century college and chapel open for visits, tours and services at certain times of day.
CAMBRIDGE & COUNTY FOLK MUSEUM - Castle Street. Tel: 01223 355159 *www.folkmuseum.org* Social history of town & gown.
MUSEUM OF TECHNOLOGY - Cheddars Lane off Newmarket Road. Tel: 01223 368650 *www.museumoftechnology.com* Victorian pumping station and associated machinery open Sunday afternoons with special steaming dates.

Boating
SCUDAMORE'S PUNTS - Mill Lane. Tel: 01223 359750 *www.scudamores.com* Chauffeured and self-hired punts. A must do, one of several punt hire companies.

Connections
BUSES - Cambridge Blue and Stagecoach operate frequent buses from outside the station into the centre. CITY SIGHTSEEING operate open top tour buses every 15-20 minutes from the station. Tel: 01708 866000 *www.city-sightseeing.com*
TAXIS - Panther. Tel: 01223 715715. Diamond - Tel: 01223 523523.
BICYCLE HIRE - Station cycles. Tel: 01223 307125. Handily placed establishment by the railway station also usefully offering left luggage facilities. Charges from £6 for half day hire to £16 per week etc.
CAR HIRE - AVA. Tel: 01223 412655.

Eccles Road
Map 6

Wayside halt largely bereft of trains.

Ely
Map 3

Haughty on its hilltop, and crowned by one of the loveliest ecclesiastical buildings in Christendom, 'Eel Island' displays a Herewardian capacity for dealing with invaders, not Normans now but tourists. Thus the hoardes are assimilated without recourse to suffocation, leaving Ely to go about its small town existence unselfconsciously, and absolved from any real need to parade itself as a honeypot.

Accommodation
THE LAMB HOTEL - Lynn Road. Tel: 01353 663574 *www.oldenglish.co.uk* Traditional 3 Star hotel located in the town centre. Bar and restaurant food for non-residents.
CATHEDRAL HOUSE - St Mary's Street. Tel: 01353 662124. Bed & breakfast in the shadow of the Cathedral.
CHAPEL COTTAGE - Chapel Street. Tel: 01353 668768. Cosy, inexpensive bed & breakfast.

Eating & Drinking
STAGECOACH RESTAURANT - Market Street. Tel: 01353 669930. Well appointed restaurant cooking with local produce.
THE MALTINGS - Ship Lane. Tel: 01353 669757. Modern extension to former riverside maltings. Choice ranges from light snacks to full meals.
THE ALMONRY - High Street. Tel: 01353 666360. Home cooking in vaulted dining rooms dating from the 12th century, spilling out into a garden beside the cathedral on warm summer days. Not open for

dinner.

PEACOCK'S TEAROOM - Waterside. Tel: 01353 661100. Quaint tearooms beside the river.

THE CUTTER - Waterside. Tel: 01353 662713. Busy riverside inn dating back to the days of the early 19th century river improvements, hence the name.

THE FOUNTAIN - Silver Street. Tel: 01353 663122. CAMRA recommended haven of calm close to the Cathedral. No meals.

Shopping

A large TESCO supermarket adjoins the railways station, but on their hilltop Ely 's shops exude a traditional air. There are good markets on Thursdays and Saturdays, the latter being a Farmer's Market on the second and fourth Saturdays monthly. Bookworms should make a bee-line for TOPPINGS excellent bookshop on the High Street (Tel: 01353 645005) a telling example of how independent bookshops can flourish given enthusiasm, care and attention to detail. Antique collectors will similarly relish WATERSIDE ANTIQUES (Tel: 01353 667066) housed in former maltings on the riverbank, whilst nearby is BABYLON GALLERY (Tel: 01353 616993) featuring regular exhibitions of work by leading modern artists.

Things to Do

TOURIST INFORMATION - Oliver Cromwell's House, St Mary's Street. Tel: 01355 662062. Located in charming half-timbered town house once occupied by Oliver Cromwell, with exhibits and tableaux relating to his life and times.

ELY CATHEDRAL - Tel: 01353 667735. The modest admission charge is a small price to pay for immersing oneself in such calm and splendour. Try and make it for Evensong at 5.30pm!

ELY MUSEUM - The Old Gaol, Market Street. Tel: 01353 666655. Well presented aspects of Ely and Fenland life from Roman times through to the Second World War.

PRICKWILLOW DRAINAGE ENGINE MUSEUM - Prickwillow, 4 miles east of Ely on B1382. Tel: 01353 688360 *www.prickwillow-engine-museum.co.uk* Fabulous shrine devoted to pumping engines and the business of keeping the Fens watertight. Worth including, perhaps, as part of the River Heritage Walk.

Walking

Ely is a useful staging post on the FEN RIVERS WAY which links King's Lynn with Cambridge. More locally RIVER HERITAGE WALKS trace the old and new courses of the Great Ouse between Ely and Littleport, the longest totalling 9 miles with a train ride thrown in. For a short introduction to the town itself try the newly developed EEL TRAIL featuring a sequence of specially commissioned artworks. Leaflets available from the TIC.

Boating

FENLAND RIVER CRUISES - Tel: 01353 777567. Half hour boat trips exploring Ely's riverfront.

Connections

TAXIS - A10 Taxis. Tel: 01353 661010. Fencabs - Tel: 01353 669966.

BICYCLE HIRE - City Cycle Centre, Market Street,. Tel: 01353 663131.

CAR HIRE - Chettisham Garage, Lynn Road. Tel: 01353 662700.

Harling Road   *Map 5*

Station for East Harling two miles to the south on the far side of the River Thet. Regrettably few trains.

Lakenheath   *Map 4*

Prospective visitors by rail to Lakenheath must contend with a skeletal train service and a three mile hike. But persistence will reveal a congenial hotel (The LAKENHEATH HOTEL - Tel: 01842 860691) a Filipino restaurant (FILIPINIANA - Tel: 01842 862660), a number of pubs, fish & chip shop, a Co-op, Post Office and a Lloyds TSB bank with cash machine. Much of Lakenheath life revolves around the American fighter base. Adjacent to the railway station there's an RSPB bird reserve - Tel: 01603 661662 *www.rspb.org.uk*

TAXIS - Phoenix. Tel: 01638 533060. Bob's - Tel: 01638 828471.

Norwich   *Maps 7, 12 & 17*

Locked in an affectionate embrace, Norwich and the Wensum have shaped and defined each other since Rouen stone was carried upriver to build the cathedral, whose soaring spire pinpoints the city for miles around. Of all English cities, arguably only York is as closely in touch with its medieval past. Thirty-two churches add weight to this theory, as does an initially bewildering street pattern. The best approach from the railway station is along the riverbank via Pulls Ferry and thence through the cathedral precincts into Tombland. In the Middle Ages Norwich was considered England's second city, its wealth built on weaving. But the rampant advance of 18th and 19th century industrialisation in the Midlands and the North relegated the city to a regional backwater. Until the railways arrived its transport links were too eastern facing to compete. Via the Wensum and the Yare it was easier for Norwich to trade with the Low Countries than with the rest of England. This regional bias moulded Norwich until road became the dominant mode of transport in the second half of the 20th century; though even now it is significant that no motorway comes within striking distance of the city. But, in essence, Norwich's insularity remains its greatest strength. It is a bewitching place, best savoured by those wise enough to arrive by rail or river.

Accommodation

MAIDS HEAD HOTEL - Tombland. Tel: 0870 6096110. Fine traditional hotel which can trace its history back to when Queen Elizabeth I stayed.

HOTEL NELSON - Prince of Wales Road. Tel: 01603 760260. Modern Three Star Swallow hotel across the road and river from the railway station. Guests have automatic entry to the hotel's leisure club and swimming pool.

Eating & Drinking

PREZZO - Thorpe Road. Tel: 01603 660404. Swift service characterises this well appointed Italian restaurant opposite the station.

OLIVES - Elm Hill. Tel: 01603 230500. Open from 8am (10am on Sundays) this comfortable coffee house/delicatessen is a haven of calm for shoppers and explorers alike. Bagels, panninis and ciabattas with a variety of fillings.

TATLERS - Tombland. Tel: 01603 766670 *www.tatlers.com* The menus may come on silver clip-boards, but the food is gold star. Closed Sundays, but otherwise this Georgian town house restaurant is open for luncheon and dinner daily.

BRITONS ARMS - Elm Hill. Tel: 01603 623367. Homely, family run coffee house and restaurant in a thatched, 15th century house. Open Mon-Sat 9.30am to 5pm. Open fires in winter and garden in summer.

JUN SHON - Riverside Quarter. Tel: 01603 611129. A magic wand has transformed this Dutch barge into a Chinese junk. Moored on the Wensum immediately opposite the railway station.

COACH & HORSES - Thorpe Road. Tel: 01603 477077. 'The first pub to visit when you arrive by train' is sound advice from the *Good Beer Guide*. Turn right outside the station and this friendly pub is inside a brisk four minutes' walk away. Beers from Norwich's own Chalk Hill Brewery and a good choice of bar food.

RIBS OF BEEF - Wensum Street. Tel: 01603 619517. 'The city's favourite local'. Up to eleven real ales on tap, riverside setting.

Shopping

Norwich boasts one of the best outdoor markets in Britain, its canvas-striped stalls ranked picturesquely beneath the City Hall. The stalls are both characterful and full of characters; eavesdropping an irresistible delight, always assuming you can penetrate the Norkie vernacular. The radiating nature of the city's streets have created an appealing tendency for shopping to be themed. So that for example in St Giles you'll come upon books and records, in Pottergate crafts, and in Lower Goat Lane clothing. In the Royal Arcade resides COLMAN'S MUSTARD SHOP which celebrates the history of this famous Norwich condiment. On London Street is JARROLD'S department store, a Norwich institution since 1823. There are good antiquarian bookshops on Tombland and Elm Hill, and there's a fine old fashioned camera shop called PHILIPS on Wensum Street.

Things to Do

TOURIST INFORMATION - The Forum. Tel: 01603 727927 *www.norwich.gov.uk*

CITY SIGHTSEEING - Tel: 01263 587005. Open top bus tours around the city hourly from April to October. Pick up point outside the railway station, hop on and off at your fancy.

CITY BOATS - Tel: 01603 701701. Boat cruises from stops adjacent to Elm Hill and the Railway Station of varying duration. A charming way to see Norwich and its hinterland from a different perspective.

ORIGINS - The Forum. Tel: 01603 727920 *www.theforumnorwich.co.uk* Local history and culture made interactive and housed in a new building which the locals nickname 'the haut-bannof' on account of its perceived likeness to a German railway station.

CASTLE MUSEUM & ART GALLERY - Castle Meadow. Tel: 01603 493636 *www.museums.norfolk.gov.uk* Art, archaeology and natural history exhibitions housed in the massive keep of a Norman castle. Fine collection of the Norwich School of painting featuring the work of John Crome, John Sell Cotman et al.

DRAGON HALL - King Street. Tel: 01603 663922 www.dragonhall.org Medieval merchants' trading hall.

STRANGERS' HALL - Charing Cross. Tel: 01603 493636 www.museums.norfolk.gov.uk Social history in a former merchant's house.

INSPIRE - St Michael's Church, Coslany Street. Tel: 01603 612612 www.science-projects.org Hands-on science in a former church.

Walking
MARRIOTT'S WAY offers twenty-one miles of traffic-free walking and cycling along the trackbed of the former Midland & Great Northern Railway, starting near the site of Norwich City station on Barn Road and ending at Aylsham where you can join the Bure Valley Path to Wroxham.

Connections
BUSES - Tel: 0870 608 2 608.
TAXIS - Five Star. Tel: 01603 455555.
CAR HIRE - Hertz. Tel: 01603 660160.
BIKE HIRE - Street Life. Tel: 01603 626660.

Shippea Hill   Map 3
Pimple-like eminence of the face of the fen where an earlier course of the Little Ouse ran past a sizeable mere lost in the geological mists of time.

Spooner Row   Map 6
Straggling hamlet reached down 'quiet lanes' off the A11. THE BOAR (Tel: 01953 605851) is a well-appointed inn offering bar and restaurant food.

Thetford   Map 5
The Little Ouse flows charmingly through Thetford, once the Saxon capital of East Anglia. Until 1930 it was the home of Burrells, manufacturers of much celebrated and admired steam traction engines and showman's engines. Overspill housing schemes increased the population in the 1960s, but Thetford still evinces all the self-effacing characteristics of a small country town. Thoughtful road layouts ensure that there is no through traffic in the town centre and so, unusually for a town of this size, you can hear yourself think as you explore points of interest, not least a substantial earthwork of Norman origin overlaying an Iron Age rampart and the ruins of a Cluniac Priory.

Accommodation
THE BELL - King Street. Tel: 01842 754455 www.oldenglish.co.uk Well appointed three star hotel in the town centre housed in former 15th century inn.

THE THOMAS PAINE HOTEL - White Hart Street. Tel: 01842 755631. Two star hotel within five minutes walk of the station. Thought to be the birthplace of the author of The Age of Reason in 1737.

WEREHAM HOUSE - White Hart Street. Tel: 01842 761956. Small private hotel close to the station.

THE WHITE HOUSE - Raymond Street. Tel: 01842 754546. Bed & Breakfast.

Eating & Drinking
MY HOME - White Hart Street. Tel: 01842 763535. Portuguese cooking, open for breakfasts (from 9.30am), lunches and dinners daily ex Mondays.

NIMMI - White Hart Street. Tel: 01842 761260. Indian restaurant opposite the Tourist Information Centre.

THE MULBERRY - Raymond Street. Tel: 01842 820099. Quaint street corner restaurant between the river and the market square.

Shopping
King Street is the main, traffic-free, thoroughfare and it plays host to a number of High Street chains such as Boots and W. H. Smith. There is a large TESCO supermarket on the eastern outskirts of town, and there are markets on Tuesdays and Saturdays.

Things to Do
TOURIST INFORMATION - White Hart Street. Tel: 01842 820689 www.explorethetford.co.uk www.brecks.org

CHARLES BURRELL MUSEUM - Minstergate. Tel: 01842 754247. Emerging museum project devoted to the history of Burrell's famous traction engines and farm machinery.

ANCIENT HOUSE MUSEUM - White Hart Street. Tel: 01842 752599. Half-timbered Tudor town house exhibiting local history. Currently under refurbishment.

Walking
The Iceni Way is an 84-mile path for ramblers linking Knettishall Heath (to the east of Thetford) with Holme next the Sea on the North Norfolk coast. The walk parallels the railway between Thetford, Brandon and Lakenheath and there are also railway connections at Downham Market (Map 10) and King's Lynn (Map 11). Thetford station also provides access to the Peddars Way. Of a more local nature, a number of trail leaflets are obtainable from the TIC on White Hart Street which will introduce you to - amongst other things - Thetford's Dad's Army connections, the radical thinker Thomas Paine's boyhood roots and the Maharajah Duleep Singh, a Sikh prince who lived in the area in Victorian times.

Connections
BUSES - connecting buses run roughly hourly down to the town centre but it really is just as easy to walk. There are useful links with Bury St Edmunds and King's Lynn - Tel: 0870 608 2 608.

TAXIS - A1. Tel: 01842 755555.

Waterbeach   Map 1
Fenland village on the west bank of the Cam much expanded down the years by infill housing, whilst an army barracks adds further activity. Facilities include several pubs, fish & chip shop, Chinese and Indian take-aways, two general stores (with cash machines) a butcher, baker and pharmacy. The station is a useful staging point for walkers on the Fen Rivers Way.

Wymondham   Map 6
The River Tiffey, a tributary of the Yare, winds prettily around the purlieus of this coquettish little town, which comes into its own on the wintry nights leading up to Christmas, when the Abbey is floodlit and there is carol singing in the Market Place. The Abbey seems massive enough still, and yet was twice the size prior to the Dissolution of 1538. A few years later 'Windam' (as it is pronounced locally) was at the centre of a rebellion against the enclosures. One of the Kett brothers was hung in chains from the abbey roof for his pains. A fire destroyed much of the town in 1615, and resulted in a new Market Cross being erected, presently and charmingly housing the Tourist Information Centre.

Accommodation
WYMONDHAM CONSORT - Market Street. Tel: 01953 606721. Two Star Best Western Hotel overlooking the Market Cross.

ABBEY HOTEL - Church Street. Tel: 01953 602148. Three Star hotel in quiet street adjacent to Abbey.

Eating & Drinking
BRIEF ENCOUNTER - railway station. Tel: 01953 606433. Superb station refreshment room open (9.30am-4pm) daily for coffees, lunches and afternoon teas - see page 19.

NUMBER TWENTY FOUR - Middleton Street. Tel: 01953 607750. Highly regarded restaurant.

RENDEZVOUS - Market Street. Tel: 01953 606721. Italian wine-bar adjunct to Consort Hotel.

CASABLANCA - Middleton Street. Tel: 01953 607071. Lively bistro.

GREEN DRAGON - Church Street. Tel: 01953 607907. Quaint half-timbered inn merely singed by the fire of 1615. Food and accommodation.

Shopping
Old fashioned enough for Early Closing to bite on Wednesdays, 'Windam' stretches from its customary torpor on Fridays for a small street market, and on the 3rd Saturday in the month for a Farmers Market, the first of its kind in the county.

Things to Do
TOURIST INFORMATION - Market Cross. Tel: 01953 604721.

HERITAGE MUSEUM - The Bridewell. Tel: 01953 600205. Open March to November. Excellent displays of local history.

MID NORFOLK RAILWAY - Tel: 01362 690633 www.mnr.org.uk Preserved 11 mile section of the former Wymondham-Dereham railway. Trains arrive and depart (Talking timetable - Tel: 01362 851723) from Wymondham Abbey station approximately 20 minutes walk from the main railway station.

LOTUS CARS - factory tours on Wednesdays only. Tel: 01953 608547.

Walking
KETT'S COUNTRY WALK - signposted walk from Wymondham to Norwich through places associated with the Rebellion of 1549.

Connections
BUSES - buses run every quarter of an hour from the station forecourt to Norwich via Wymondham town centre (10 minutes walk away) and Hethersett. Tel: 0870 608 2 608.

TAXIS - Station Taxis. Tel: 01953 600007. Ron's Taxis - Tel: 01953 601050.

The FEN Line

IT is a poor pun, but on the surface of it - the flat, featureless *surface* of it - the twenty-six miles between Ely and King's Lynn do not have much going for them, either for tourists or those of a railway bent. Yet there is more to the 'Fen Line' than meets the mitigated eye. The Fenlands, with their black soils and silvery drains, may be an acquired taste, but as Dodie Smith's heroine Cassandra Mortmain put it in *I Capture the Castle*, 'flat country seems to give the sky such a chance'.

Pacing up and down on Ely's often windswept station for the King's Lynn connection, you may well be inclined to reflect that the sky grabs its chance almost too gleefully. Yet there are elements of residual dignity in the station architecture which encourage your gaze to fall into focus. Moreover, the timetable provides a never less than interesting procession of passenger and freight trains from all corners of the railway compass which help to make the time pass quickly.

Traditionally, through trains from London to King's Lynn - a distance of just under ninety-seven miles - ran from Liverpool Street. Since the route was electrified in 1992, however, all but a handful of rush hour services have run to and from King's Cross. City types may bridle at the shift in emphasis, theatre-goers prefer the easy access which King's Cross offers to the West End. Enthusiasts are more likely to mourn the withdrawal of locomotive-hauled trains. In steam days trains were split at Ely into portions for Norwich and

King's Lynn, the latter making their way across the Fens behind Holden 4-4-0s or 4-6-0s or Gresley B17s. In diesel days English Electric Type 3s and Brush Type 4s took the strain; they served a peerless brand of Tomato Soup in the Buffet Car, and there was poetry in their loping progress under Dodie Smith skies. For the most part now, Fen Line services are provided by WAGN Class 365 electric units - sleek, swift and, well, dull. But if the trains lack charisma, the railway positively oozes with it. Don't let the flat, diminishing landscape render you trance-like. Concentrate, and let the Fenlands unveil their spell.

Departing from Ely, it is simple to differentiate between the tourist and the train-spotter: the former will be hypnotized by the Cathedral, the latter entranced by Potter's freight terminal, opened on the site of a former sugar beet factory (closed in 1980) and now flourishing as an excellent example of how goods, all too often surrendered to road, can be won back to rail. Major commodities dealt with at Ely include chipboard and paper. Containerised goods, imported from East Coast ports, are increasingly handled here for onward distribution to the Midlands. The Potter Group also have railheads at Selby in Yorkshire and Knowsley on Merseyside.

The sugar beet works that predated Potters was opened in 1925. It employed both rail and water transport. Coal was brought in by barge up the Great Ouse from King's Lynn docks. Sugar beet was carried by barge from many farms in the district. The barges employed were built of steel. In earlier days Fen Lighters would have traded on the river, owing their origins to the construction of Denver Sluice in the 17th century, which effectively prevented sea-going vessels from trading inland. The Fen Lighters were worked in 'trains' of up to half a dozen barges, alternately being powered by sail or horse. They plied the Ouse and its tributaries in large numbers until the railways came.

As the lines to Peterborough and Norwich splay out into infinities of fen, the King's Lynn line forges northward, accompanying the high-banked Great Ouse, inscrutably invisible from the train. This straight course of the river dates from 1830. The Light Blues of Cambridge University use this length for training in the confidence that no Dark Blue spies can watch unobserved. It is not widely known that in 1944 the University Boat Race was actually held between the River Lark's entrance into the Ouse and Queen Adelaide. Five thousand people turned out to watch the event on a bitterly cold February day, local

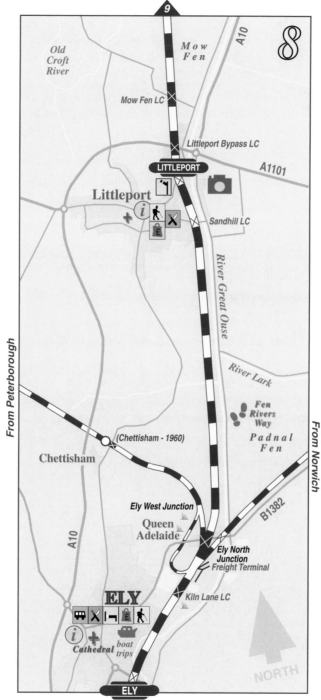

spectators boosted by numerous soldiers and airmen from military camps in the vicinity. The crews rowed downstream from Ely to reach the start. Despite being on home ground, Cambridge lost by three quarters of a length. In 2004 the race was re-enacted to mark the sixtieth anniversary of this curious piece of sporting history and Cambridge gained their revenge watched by six veterans of the original encounter.

Another water sport has close associations with the area. In 1892 a local philanthropist purchased land alongside the railway to create a forty acre skating ground, and over the next few years Littleport became a popular venue for ice skating competitions - in 1900 the Professional Championship of Great Britain was held here. On occasion excursion trains were stabled in sidings to the south of the station to give their occupants a grandstand view of the proceedings.

At LITTLEPORT there was once an interchange dock affording the facility of transhipment of goods between the river and the railway. Hay was boated in from waterside farms for transhipment into railway wagons, whilst Nottinghamshire and Yorkshire coal travelled in the opposite direction, being loaded on to barges for onward carriage to the pumping engines. The dock now provides moorings for pleasure craft.

Beyond Littleport the line was singled, as far as Downham Market, in 1984. The river bears off in a north-easterly direction along a reach known locally as Hemmings Eau, originally dug by the Romans. Meanwhile the train embarks upon the next stage of the journey, traversing farmland drained not only of water, but of humanity also.

These are the harsh landscapes familiar to the Littleport Rioters of 1816. Fuelled by drink, a large group of farm labourers ransacked various shops and houses in the town and confronted a particularly unpopular landowner. They were quietened with false offers of cheaper flour and higher wages, but not entirely satisfied marched on Ely where all their demands appeared to be met, along with the disarming offer of free beer. Mollified they returned home only to be hunted down the following day by a force of foot soldiers, cavalry and Bow Street Runners. In the ensuing fracas three soldiers were injured but two labourers killed and almost a hundred arrested. They were tried by the so called 'Hanging Judge of Wisbech', one Edward Christian, brother of Fletcher, the *Bounty* mutineer. Nineteen were transported to Botany Bay for life and five were hung, publically, at Ely.

ACCORDING to Sir Harry Godwin, 'To travel by train north from Ely is to be reminded of the vast Hungarian plain'. Septuagenarian Emeritus Professor of Botany at Cambridge University when he wrote that, it is obviously not a spurious or merely romanticised analogy. You may draw your own comparisons. These big wide vistas are conducive to expansive thought processes.

For a while the Great Ouse withdraws into the middle distance. At Black Horse Drove you cross from Cambridgeshire into Norfolk. There was a signal box and siding here for many years. A level crossing remains on the by-road to Cold Harbour Farm; Fenland nomenclature resonates with the bleak, watery aspect of the countryside. Southery Fen had a siding too, and at one time a horse-drawn narrow gauge train trundled across the surrounding farmland to bring agricultural produce to the main line for onward transit.

HILGAY station lay more than two miles to the south-west of the village of the same name, a statistic which eloquently explains its absence from the timetable now. Possibly this is the 'Hockwell' of the Graham Swift's novel *Waterland*, whose narrator likens the night time noise of trains for King's Lynn and Ely to baying monsters. And whilst he acknowledges the landscape's 'unrelieved and monotonous flatness' and its propensity for encouraging 'fruitless meditations on the law of perspective', he is far from immune to its 'fairy-tale' atmosphere. Celery, carrots and potatoes used to be dispatched from Hilgay overnight for sale the next morning at London's Covent Garden. Just before the Second World War broke out, a train collided with a lorry here and four people died as a result. Level crossing accidents are nothing new.

Although the Ely to King's Lynn railway is largely, and understandably, free from significant gradients, it does climb briefly, to the north of Hilgay, in order to make a crossing of the rivers Ouse and Wissey and the neighbouring Cut-Off Channel, via which, water is pumped to Essex for domestic use. The Ouse since you last encountered it, has been boosted by its navigable tributary, the Little Ouse.

When the line was opened there was a small wayside station on the south bank of the River Ouse with the peculiar spelling of 'Ouze Bridge'. The present girder bridge dates from 1906, its wide trackbed betraying the fact that the line was once double throughout. The Wissey, spanned by a less remarkable girder bridge, rises near Bradenham and essays a thirty mile

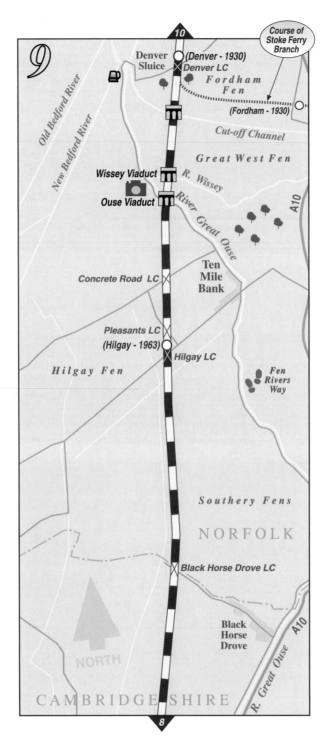

course to its confluence with the Ouse. Skirting Breckland, it hardly encounters any settlement of note before reaching Stoke Ferry, once the terminus of a branch line from Denver. Opened in 1882, passenger trains ceased running two years short of the line's half century. Not a great innings, but a useful one.

On the horizon to the east stands Wissington's sugar beet works, said to be the largest in Europe. During the 'campaigns' of autumn and winter the plumes of white steam issuing from its chimneys might fancifully be mistaken for a distant steam train. Fancifully nowadays that is, but once the works operated no less than eighteen miles of light railway tracks, a network fanning out from the sugar factory itself to remote fenland sidings at which the beet would be loaded manually on to wagons for transporting to the massive plant. One of the system's saddle tanks, a 1938 vintage Hudswell Clark named *Wissington*, resides in preservation on the North Norfolk Railway. The sugar factory also employed water transport. Tugs hauled 'trains' of barges carrying coal to feed the furnaces from the docks at Lynn, and sugar beet from waterside farms.

Back on the main line, DENVER station closed on the same day that the Stoke Ferry branch lost its passenger services; though you can still see its platform faces in the undergrowth. Freight, however, continued to use the branch for many years after: until 1965 as far as Stoke Ferry itself, and until the early 1980s to and from the sugar beet works. A notable landmark to the east is Denver Windmill, used continually from its construction in 1835 until the sails were struck by lightning during the Second World War, but now happily fully restored and open to the public.

At Denver Sluice the Old and New Bedford Rivers - 17th century drainage channels dug by the pre-eminent Dutch engineer Cornelius Vermuyden - rejoin the Ouse, having parted company with it in the vicinity of Earith, halfway between Ely and Huntingdon. Without such artificial cuts the Fenland landscape would be very different indeed - swamp and marsh for the main part. But in addition to their contribution to drainage and flood control, these channels are also navigable, and though hardly as popular as the midland canals or Norfolk Broads, there are devotees of the Great Ouse and its tributaries and the Middle Level Navigations (which provide a link between the Ouse and the Nene) who derive considerable satisfaction from exploring The Fens by boat - even if they experience some difficulty in seeing over the flood banks!

DOWNHAM MARKET is the most significant settlement between Ely and King's Lynn. The track redoubles as your train slows to negotiate two level-crossings, the second overlooked by a large flour mill and controlled from a handsome timber signal box, made all the more charming by its deep eaves and daintily scalloped bargeboards. But if you're taken with the signal box, wait 'til you see the station! Railway architecture expert Gordon Biddle has called it 'cosy', and you cannot help but concur. Constructed from local carstone, bolstered by yellow brick quoins around its doors and windows and corners, it is the Jacobean gables and lofty chimneys which lend it such a unselfconsciously prepossessing air. How fine it must feel to have this as your local station, more so when you pass through the entrance doors to discover not only a staffed booking hall but an utterly charming little refreshment room to boot. Wouldn't it be good if all small town stations were like this? But when you ensconce yourself in one of the deep armchairs which the proprietor, Andrew Archibald, thoughtfully provides for his clientele, and try to conjure up a list of peers, it is difficult to think beyond the likes of Great Malvern, Dingwall, Crediton and nearby Wymondham (Map 6). So you wouldn't need a 'short list' for awards in this category!

Passenger trains are usually timetabled to pass on the double track section between Downham Market and Watlington, echoes of the route's main line status in years gone by, when the journey could have been made in a buffet car express from Liverpool Street. What price a trip now on *The Fenman* which used to leave Hunstanton at the unearthly hour of quarter to seven in the morning, run all stations to King's Lynn (where it reversed) proceed to Ely (where it picked up a portion from Wisbech and March) and continue to Cambridge (where it picked up another portion from Bury St Edmunds and Newmarket) before finally arriving in London just short of ten o'clock. Nowadays, if you're lucky, the through journey from Hunstanton to London by public transport might shave half an hour off *The Fenman's* overall schedule, but it involves a change from bus to train at King's Lynn (and a five minute walk between the respective termini of the two modes of transport) and you will not be able to partake of a hot breakfast of eggs and bacon in the buffet car on the way up to Town!

With the Great Ouse and its Relief Channel to the west

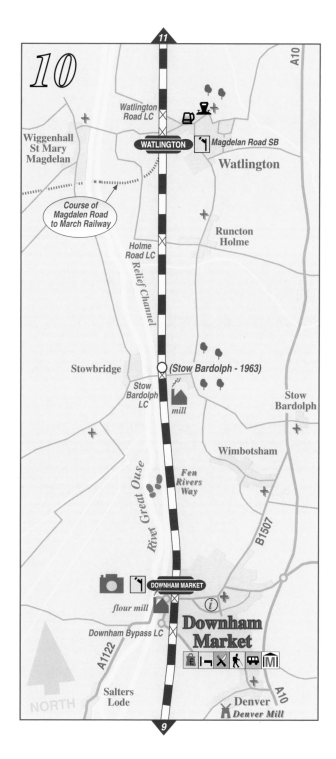

and archetypal fenland fields to the east, the railway continues in a largely level, largely straight trajectory, northbound. On the approach to STOW BARDOLPH you encounter another mill, this one engaged in the production of animal feeds. The surroundings, unfortunately, betray that regrettable rural trait of untidiness, rusting and abandoned machinery marring the lineside view as though you were on the squalid outskirts of some hideous industrial town. The original wayside station here (whose buildings remain in domestic use) was known simply as Stow. When, however, the mighty London & North Eastern Railway took over from the Great Eastern at the Grouping in 1923, it was decided to add the suffix Bardolph to avoid any possible confusion with the old North British Railway station of Stow, 356 miles away in Midlothian by the shortest rail route, also at that moment absorbed into the LNER system.

WATLINGTON is another Fenland railway station which has undergone a change of name, or rather reverted in this instance to its original. For many years it was known - somewhat more poetically perhaps - as Magdelan Road. Here was the junction for a single track branch line which sliced across the fens to Wisbech before dog-legging down to March. A useful route in the wider scheme of things which succumbed post-Beeching in 1968. Collateral damage saw Magdalen Road lose its passenger trains with abandonment of the Wisbech line, but it was resurrected, after a lapse of seven years, to the delight of the inhabitants of the burgeoning village of Watlington, whose name it re-adopted in 1989. The down platform is original, the up a staggered replacement on the north side of the level crossing. Curiously, the signal box retains the name Magdelan Road.

Arthur Randell, author of *Fenland Railwayman* (Routledge & Kegan Paul, 1968), is doubtless looking down from heaven with approval. His book lyrically evoked the working practices of Magdelan Road in the years before and during the Great War: the three eight-hour shifts; loading milk churns on to the London express; driving recalcitrant cattle and sheep on to goods trains for the shorter journey to the Tuesday Market at Lynn; attending to 'The Mail' before it made an habitually explosive departure for London at two in the morning; and dealing with every conceivable commodity from foxhound dung to freshly caught eels as the railway, the country's 'common carrier' was required to do in those days.

ON single track again, the train proceeds on the last lap of your Fenland journey to King's Lynn. Beyond St German's level-crossing it spans the River Nar, an unnavigable tributary which basks in the reputation of being one of the county's loveliest watercourses, especially when viewed in the neighbourhood of Castle Acre where it is crossed by the Peddars Way. By the time it reaches the Ely-King's Lynn railway it has lost much of its youthful charm. Aesthetically, matters might have been much worse had the discovery of oil in the vicinity in the 1920s developed as spectacularly as its optimistic proponents had hoped.

These were the self-styled English Oilfields. A siding was laid out in a graceful trailing curve from Clarke's Drove to serve the installation's retorts and appurtenances. An eager workforce assembled off the land, farmworkers who sensed they might strike it rich in the rush for 'black gold', a long awaited opportunity to throw off generations of feudal toil. Their enthusiasm was shortlived. What oil there was contained a high sulphur content which didn't endear it to end users. Drilling ceased in the Thirties.

In their heyday, railways lines converged on King's Lynn from five directions. Furthermore there were goods lines into the harbour and the docks which served to increase the sense of round-the-clock activity. The accompanying map can only hint at these complexities, but as the train loses speed and you begin to encounter the outskirts of the town, you might catch a glimpse of an old bridge abutment, a melancholy remnant of the Midland & Great Northern Railway which skirted the southern edge of Lynn on its way east to Melton Constable and beyond. Through trains from the midlands to the east coast called at the M&GN's undistinguished station at South Lynn, travellers to the town centre being provided with a push & pull shuttle service which traversed the curve to Harbour Junction before continuing into King's Lynn along the main line. Little trace of South Lynn's railways remain, but the cylindrical piers of the river bridge are still there, whilst part of the trackbed of the M&GN eastwards has become the site of a traveller's camp.

The Harbour Branch departed from the main line just to the north of where the A47 by-pass spans the railway now. Some trackwork remains, disconsolately curving away in both directions, though it is evident from its rusty condition that no goods trains have passed this way for many a year.

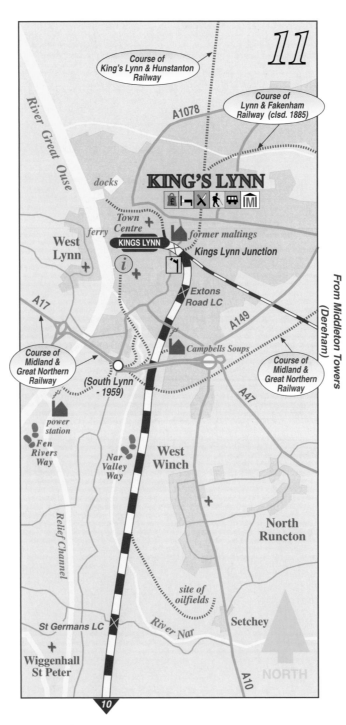

The last time the Harbour Branch was used seems to have been around 1990. The line crossed the River Nar and Mill Fleet upon a pair of Heath Robinsonesque swing-bridges and stretched as far as King's Staithe on the south bank of the Pur Fleet. One of the last local users of rail freight was Campbells Soups. Their tall premises remain a landmark on the east side of the line where the by-pass crosses it. They were keen advocates of rail transport until the early Nineties, by which time British Rail were actively discouraging wagon-load freight. Happily, when the trackwork from Campbells sidings was lifted it found a new lease of life on the North Norfolk Railway.

Industry gives way to lineside allotments as the train slows for the terminus. Pockets of newer housing are followed by terraced Victorian streets. Birch saplings on apparent wasteland are all that remain of a curving phalanx of sidings once used as a necessary overflow to the town's main goods yard. At King's Lynn Junction another line comes in from the east. This lost its passenger trains on the same sad September day in 1968 as the Magdelan Road-Wisbech-March line. At a stroke of Beeching's unforgiving axe, the public could no longer travel directly from King's Lynn to March or Dereham and Norwich by train. No doubt the Dereham line would have been ripped up entirely had it not been for the prolific sand pits at Middleton Towers, three miles east of Lynn. Forty years on the line is still used to convey sand in hopper wagons to glassworks in Yorkshire, the last rail-born freight of any description to use the Fen Line.

The final, regrettably absent piece of King's Lynn's railway jigsaw is the line which once continued northwards to the seaside resort of Hunstanton. It contrived to eke out a further eight months of life following the demise of the Dereham and Wisbech routes, closing in the May of the following year just as passenger figures might have been expected to increase for the summer season. John Betjeman travelled over it in 1962, relishing the view ahead through the diesel railcar's front windows with his uniquely contagious enthusiasm and making a charming travelogue of the journey in the process. The train ride took half an hour with five intermediate stops. Today's bus service takes fifty minutes.

From one Poet Laureate to another! So prepare to shed 'tears, idle tears' as the Fen Line crosses Tennyson Avenue

under the watchful eye of a sizeable signal box. A run-round loop, located on the now abandoned line into the docks, enables the sand train to reverse. You can watch it go through the motions at about a quarter to nine in the morning while your 'other half' shops in the Morrisons and Matalan stores recently erected on the site of King's Lynn goods yard. It goes without saying that neither shop receives its incoming goods by rail. Frequently, these days, retail outlets are established on former railway land, and one would have thought some form of coercion should be applied by the planning authorities involved to encourage the use of rail in these circumstances.

The line round to the Alexander and Bentinck docks, though still in situ, has lain unused for over a decade, apparently not so much because it was obsolete and unwanted but because it was unclear who owned it. A large malthouse, converted into flats, views this inertia with appropriate disdain. Once it also overlooked a four-road engine shed and turntable (31C to aficionados) the home depot, down the years, of locomotives kept specially burnished for the haulage of Royal Trains to and from Wolferton (for Sandringham) on the Hunstanton line.

Considering that it has lost so many services, KING'S LYNN station has survived remarkably well. Its long island platforms stretch out to greet you with the tell-tale eagerness of an elderly aunt who doesn't get as many visitors as she used to; an aunt, however, remarkably well-preserved for her age and still with all her mental faculties about her. In other words the station remains staffed and its delightful timber-clad tea rooms continue to provide solace and sustenance for wayfarers all. Out through the entrance doors and over the road stands a pub called The Fenman, an alternative establishment to end your journey amidst sundry railwayana and archive photographs of Lynn's railway in its smoky heyday. If only they sold Claud Hamilton bitter ...

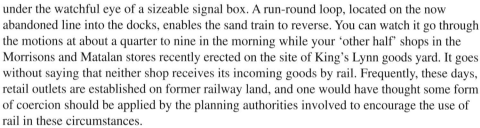

Gazetteer

Ely
See page 21.

Maps 3 & 8

Downham Market
Map 10

A quiet, old-fashioned market town where the Fens give way to rolling Norfolk farmland. Half a dozen miles to the north-east lies Marham aerodrome, the second largest RAF installation in the UK. Downham's best known feature is the cast iron clock tower in the market place, gifted to the town by a local businessman in 1878, and whilst it looks as though it might have escaped from some Birmingham suburb or other, it certainly stamps its seal of approval on the town centre. In earlier days, Downham was famous for its buttermarket - two thousand firkins per week - a wholesale operation which saw butter being delivered by barge along the Great Ouse, prior to onward transportation southwards. By the time it reached London it was more urbanely (if innaccurately and unfairly) marketed as 'Cambridge Butter'. Charles I is said to have stayed here disguised as a clergyman following his defeat at Naseby in 1646, and Nelson is said to have attended school here. More corroboratively, two men were hanged following riots in the town in 1816, unrest which owed its origins to the same inequalities experienced in nearby Littleport.

Accommodation
CASTLE HOTEL - High Street. Tel: 01366 384311. Two Star hotel in town centre.
CHESTNUT VILLA - Railway Road. Tel: 01366 384099. Bed & Breakfast a hundred yards up the road from the station.

Eating & Drinking
FENLAND EXPRESS - railway station. Tel: 01366 386636. Great little refreshment room - coffees, teas, hot snacks, cakes etc - quaintly furnished. Gifts and crafts and souvenirs for sale and a post office counter too. Heartily recommended.
DOWNHAM FRYER - Bridge Street. Tel: 01366 383029. Take-away or eat in fish & chips ten minutes uphill from the station.
PALMERS - High Street. Tel: 01366 388124. Convivial little brasserie open for lunch and dinner Monday to Saturday.
SZECHUAN INN - Railway Road. Tel: 01366 387790. Chinese restaurant handily placed for the station but closed on Mondays.

Shopping
Downham's historical markets are held on Fridays and Saturdays. There are a number of antiques outlets and a secondhand bookshop. Somerfield and Tesco have supermarkets in the town centre.

Things to Do
TOURIST INFORMATION - Priory Centre. Tel: 01366 387440.
DENVER WINDMILL - Tel: 01366 384009 *www.denvermill.co.uk* Splendidly restored tower mill with four sails, an ogee cap and a fantail located just over a mile south of Downham town centre.

Visitor centre, shop and cafe. Telephone for details of their scheduled milling weekends and other events. Also of interest nearby is Denver Sluice.
COLLECTORS WORLD - Hermitage Hall. Tel: 01366 383185 *www.collectors-world.org* Delightfully eccentric accumulation of themed collectibles. Located on west bank of Great Ouse approximately half a mile from the railway station.
WELNEY WILDFOWL & WETLANDS CENTRE - Tel: 01353 860711 *www.wwt.org.uk/visit/welney* Though approximately 10 miles south-west of Downham (via Denver and Ten Mile Bank), this excellent visitor centre is worth drawing to the attention of rail travellers. It is located on the Hundred Foot Washes between the New and Old Bedford rivers, a vital feeding and nesting site for thousands of waterbirds. Welney is especially well known as the winter home for upwards of eight thousand Whooper and Bewick's swans.

Walking
Downham is on the Black Fen Waterway Trail and the Fen Rivers Way.

Connections
BUSES - the excellence of the rail service renders buses running north and south largely for locals only, but there is a useful service to/from March whose destination blind reads somewhat evocatively 'Three Holes for March'. Tel: 0870 608 2 608.
TAXIS - Barry's Cars. Tel: 01366 383030. Brian's Taxis. Tel: 01366 388893.

Lynn Ferry

King's Lynn
Map 11

History trips over itself in Lynn, eager to capture your attention. They were importing Baltic timber here in the Middle Ages. Nowadays it still arrives, unloaded off-river in docks built during Victoria's reign. Prior to that, Lynn's maritime commerce was conducted more colourfully in a network of creeks flowing off from the main channel - Purfleet, Millfleet and Fisherfleet - and this was once perhaps the second most important port in the kingdom. Self sufficiency guru, John Seymour, called King's Lynn 'the most romantic town in England', and the more you get to know its secret corners, the

more you begin to share his enthusiasm.

Persevere, therefore, with the initially dispiriting walk from the station to the town centre. Lynn is at its best beyond its High Street. The closer to the river you come, the more enchanting it gets. By the time you've hit on Saturday Market you're positively purring. Here stands the Parish Church of St Margaret's. It boasts two towers and two clocks, or at least you think it does until you look more closely and see that one of them tells the *tides*, not the time. In nearby side streets which, apart from the odd parked car, look little changed from the Middle Ages, you find the former homes of wealthy merchants and a warehouse once stuffed to the gills with goods traded by the Hanseatic League. Nearby looms Greyfriars Tower (a recent participant in BBC Television's *Restoration* competition) the surviving remnant of a Franciscan Friary, retained following the Dissolution as a landmark for shipping.

Alleyways lead to the riverfront, and there's the Great Ouse, flowing for three hours and ebbing for nine, and consequently never quite still. Onomatopoeically resonating with its name, the water oozes back and forth, bearing flotsam and jetsam which you can't keep up with, no matter how brisk your walking pace. Trade has deserted these quays, but left a legacy of handsome architecture, as exemplified by Henry Bell's almost perfectly symmetrical Custom House, built in 1685 from Northamptonshire stone, carried by water to King's Lynn. King Street leads you on (though don't ignore Ferry Lane) to the wide open expanse of Tuesday Market Place, dominated by the Corn Exchange, and by now you're fully smitten. What time is the *last* train home?

Accommodation
DUKES HEAD HOTEL - Tuesday Market Place. Tel: 01553 774996 *www.elizabethhotels.co.uk* Pink-faced Georgian pile designed by Henry Bell of Custom House fame. Now part of the Elizabeth Hotels Group.
THE GLOBE HOTEL - Tuesday Market Place. Tel: 01553 668000 *www.jdwetherspoonlodges.co.uk* J. D. Wetherspoon Lodge accommodation overlooking a handsome square.
STUART HOUSE HOTEL - Goodwins Road. Tel: 01553 772169 *www.stuart-house-hotel.co.uk* Well appointed, family run, Two Star hotel a walk across a park away from the town and station. CAMRA recommended bar and restaurant open to non residents.
THE OLD RECTORY - Goodwins Road. Tel: 01553 768544 *www.theoldrectory-kingslynn.com* Guest accommodation in charming Georgian house. Owner happy to meet guests arriving by train at the station.
YOUTH HOSTEL ASSOCIATION - College Lane. Tel: 01553 772461. 16th century bunk-house accommodation adjoing the banks of the Ouse.

Eating & Drinking
FENMAN - Blackfriars Road (opposite the rly sta). Tel: 01553 761889. Friendly (if smoky) CAMRA recommended local dispensing Adnams and Greene King across the road from the station. Some choice items of local railwayana decorate the walls.
RIVERSIDE RESTAURANT - King Street. Tel: 01553 773134 *www.riversiderestaurant.com* You can see the river through the

windows of this fine restaurant and on warm days they serve meals on the terrace outside.

PREZZO - Tuesday Market Place. Tel: 01553 777616. Smart Italian restaurant, part of a chain which also has a branch in Norwich.

NO.3 - Tuesday Market Place. Tel: 01553 710000. Coffee shop, wine bar and restaurant opposite the parish church.

Shopping

Chain stores in the pedestrianised High Street, markets on Tuesdays, Fridays and Saturdays, and a Morrisons supermarket alongside the station. Gift shops and galleries are, as yet, in apparently short supply, which is not to denigrate those which do exist, but rather to point out that Lynn does not yet appear to flaunt its romantic atmosphere. Great butcher's shop called PRIORS (Tel: 01553 773677) in *West* Lynn, a good excuse for using the ferry.

Things to Do

TOURIST INFORMATION - Custom House, Purfleet Quay. Tel: 01553 763044 *www.visitwestnorfolk.com* Located in the divine 17th century Custom House designed by Henry Bell. You can go upstairs and learn of the daring exploits of Captain George Vancouver who charted the west coast of North America and gave his name to the Canadian city and state, or delve into the history of the Hanseatic League and Customs & Excise.

WASH DISCOVERY CENTRE - Green Quay. Tel: 01553 818500 *www.thegreenquay.co.uk* Flora and fauna of The Wash interpreted in former riverside warehouse. Gift shop and nice waterfront cafe too.

TRUE'S YARD - North Street. Tel: 01553 770479. Fishing Heritage Museum located in what was Lynn's North End fishing community. Tea room and gift shop.

OLD GAOL HOUSE - Saturday Market Place. Tel: 01553 774297. Waxworks of Lynn's malefactors through history in dungeons beneath the 15th century Guildhall.

LYNN MUSEUM - Market Street. Tel: 01553 775001 *www.museums.norfolk.gov.uk* Local history comes to life from Roman times to Victoria and beyond.

TOWN HOUSE - Queen Street. Tel: 01553 773450 *www.museums.norfolk.gov.uk* Reconstructed rooms and tableaux from the Middle Ages to the middle Fifties.

WEST LYNN FERRY - runs every twenty minutes between 7am and 6pm (continuously at morning and evening 'rush' hours, Monday to Saturday. 50p each way and a bargain as such. Unique views of the waterfront and some interesting displays regarding the ferry's long history in the waiting room on the West Lynn side. Tel: 01553 766029 or 07974 260639

Walking

A MARITIME TRAIL leaflet is obtainable from the TIC, a prerequisite for exploring the town on foot. Of lengthier duration, the FEN RIVERS WAY runs 50 miles from King's Lynn to Cambridge with several useful railway stations en route at which to break the journey. From West Lynn the PETER SCOTT WAY leads down the west bank of the Great Ouse to the Wash and round to the mouth of the Nene where the famous naturalist once inhabited a disused lighthouse.

George Vancouver and King's Lynn's Custom House

Connections

BUSES - First services 410-3 link Lynn with Hunstanton (aka Sunny Hunny) and thence the North Norfolk Coast. X1 runs half hourly Mon-Sat and hourly Sun from Peterborough railway station to Lowestoft via Wisbech, King's Lynn, Dereham, Norwich and Yarmouth thereby replicating railway services swept away by Beeching. Tel: 0870 608 2 608.

TAXIS - Station Taxis. Tel: 01553 777788.

CAR HIRE - Enterprise. Tel: 01553 661200.

Littleport *Map 8*

Little town with a big heart, exuding a strong sense of community. Call in at The Barn information office (Tel: 01353 860449) and they'll present you with an informative and comprehensive Welcome Pack. Littleport sits astride the old Roman Road known as Akeman Street, but the most memorable episode in its history was the Riot of 1816, the culmination of growing unrest during a period of economic depression following the Napoleonic Wars. Apart from Fenland agriculture, local industry was largely restricted to a clothing factory, established initially in 1882 for the manufacture of shirts and collars, in later years prior to its closure in 1998 it made Burberry's famous trench coats. On the Church Green there's a sculpture in stainless steel of a Harley-Davidson 'Knucklehead' motorcycle of 1937. William Harley was born in Littleport in 1835 but emigrated to America at the age of 25 where he fought in the Civil War. His son, William Sylvester, founded the motor cycle company along with Arthur Davidson in 1903.

Eating & Drinking

FEN HOUSE RESTAURANT - Lynn Road. Tel: 01353 860645. Fine dining on Friday and Saturday evenings in a building once known as the Railway Tavern.

ANN'S TEA ROOM - Main Street. Tel: 01353 860462. Quaint cafe in the centre.

THE BLACK HORSE - Sandhill. Tel: 01353 860328. Riverside pub about ten minutes walk south of the station.

Shopping

Small market on Tuesdays. Small but useful range of shops in the centre about five minutes walk from the station. Nice old fashioned hardware shop called Adams. Barclays Bank with cash machine.

Walking

A couple of delightfully produced local trail leaflets (obtainable from The Barn, Adams Hardware or the Library) take as their theme Littleport's rioters, skaters and Harley-Davidson links. Each walk is only one or two miles long and can thus be easily enjoyed between trains. The station is also a useful staging point on the Fen Rivers Way.

Connections

TAXIS - Fencabs. Tel: 01353 669966.

Watlington *Map 10*

Wayside station chiefly of significance to residents of the much expanded village of the same name, but also of interest as a railhead for those intent on walking along the banks of the Great Ouse, perhaps to see the ruined church at Wiggenhall St Peter. Facilities in Watlington itself are restricted to a post office stores and a pub called The Angel - Tel: 01553 811326.

The
BITTERN
Line

VOTED 'Station of the Year' in the National Rail
Awards for 2004, the terminus station once known as
Norwich 'Thorpe' is still recognisably the setting for
the opening scene of Dick and Dorothea Callum's
Broadland adventures in Arthur Ransome's classic
children's tale of 1934, *Coot Club*. Essentially, only
the motive power and the rolling stock have altered in
appearance since Tom Dudgeon leapt aboard their
departing train and set in motion a story that has captured
the imagination of children of all ages ever since.
Ransome had been inspired to set his book on the
Broads following a three week holiday aboard a yacht
hired from a boat yard at Wroxham, an activity that
the railways had done much to foster.

Nowadays the railway's promotional energies have
a different focus. The great majority of Broadland
boaters arrive and depart by road in the 21st century,
so the emphasis has migrated away from holiday boating
in the direction of day trips. Known now as the Bittern
Line, the thirty mile route from Norwich to the seaside
resorts of Cromer and Sheringham is no longer as shy
and retiring as its avian namesake. On the contrary,

though no longer graced by such illustrious named trains as *The Broadsman* or *The Norfolkman*, the line currently boasts a more intensive service than it has ever done, being equally popular with commuters and tourists.

You enter Norwich station through an elegant *porte cochere* behind and above which rises a distinguished zinc dome. Red brick dressed with Bath stone, architecturally this is one of the great termini of the provinces. Inside, a bustling concourse of shops and cafes leads to six platform faces - three 'islands' protected from the East Anglian elements by handsome canopies. Liverpool Street expresses bustle haughtily to and from the central platforms, pushed and pulled by powerful Class 90 electric locomotives. Hourly services operated by diesel units link Norwich with Cambridge, the Midlands and the North West. Locals generally depart from the outer platforms, cautiously negotiating the station throat before making their way past the Trowse triangle and Crown Point maintenance depot. In the golden age of steam, crack expresses between London and the North Norfolk coast would use the Trowse-Wensum chord to avoid the inconvenience of calling at Norwich at all.

'They crossed a bridge, and there was the river on both sides of the line, the old river on the left curving round by the village of Thorpe with crowds of yachts and motor boats tied up under the gardens, and, on the right, a straight ugly cutting.' Thus did Ransome describe the train's escape from Norwich, a picture hardly changed but for a reduction in the number of yachts as opposed to cabin cruisers. Neither is the man made river channel (dug when the railway was built) to your right strictly 'ugly' in most eyes; reed-fringed, boat-filled backwaters, shaded by willow trees, hint at Broadland scenes to come. Whitlingham's willows were once much sought after by cricket bat manufacturers: Whitlingham's willowy landscape was once the inspiration for a number of the Norwich School of artists.

At Whitlingham Junction the *Wherry Lines* to Great Yarmouth and Lowestoft diverge and the *Bittern Line* veers steeply away in a northerly direction as if suddenly remembering its destination. Getting to grips with the gradient, the diesel climbs through a sandy cutting, shrugging off the suburbs and making for open country. Construction of the Cromer line was not as straightforward as its promoters

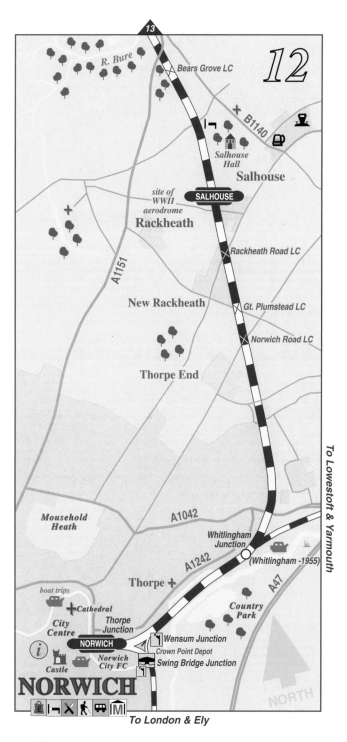

hoped. Though work began in 1865, it coincided with the collapse of the bankers Overend & Gurney and a difficult decade followed as several attempts were made to refinance the scheme. Nowadays we look glibly back in the assumption that Victorian entrepreneurs simply indentified the need for a railway and built it, whereas the reality had much more in common with the often considerably-extended and under-budgeted civil engineering projects of today.

A trio of level crossings, all guarded by automated half barriers, heralds SALHOUSE, the first stop on the line. On the up side, a quaint brick-built waiting room sheltered by a simple flat-roofed canopy, is the only building which remains. Timber built in contrast, the main station offices stood on the down side, but have been demolished. Goods facilities were restricted to a loop to the south of the station on the down side in an area now used for parking cars. Traffic in passengers and goods would have been light, at least until the Second World War and the construction of a military aerodrome in the adjacent parish of Rackheath.

The USAAF airbase at Rackheath was a relative latecomer - the first aeroplane didn't land until March, 1944. The unit came under the command of an exceptional young airman called Colonel Albert Shower. He was just thirty-five when he first arrived at Rackheath, but forty-five years later he was still spritely enough to return and unveil a memorial in the village. A memorial very much deserved, for the USAAF Bomb Group 467 - nicknamed the 'Rackheath Aggies' - had flown a total of two hundred and twelve missions in their B-24s by the time the war was over, and enjoyed a reputation for being the most accurate bombers in the Eighth Air Force.

When Alexander Frater journeyed along this line in the early Eighties, gathering copy for *Stopping Train Britain*, his driver, Reg Reynolds, reminisced about the Late Night Troop Special which left Norwich for Cromer every Saturday night after the Hippodrome had closed. From the Hippodrome to the Aerodrome and then off into the skies over Germany. Mr Reynolds particularly recalled an aeroplane called 'F for Freddie' whose crew would habitually wave at passing trains. After each mission they would paint a white bomb on the nose of the plane. They got to seventeen before they disappeared.

Beyond Salhouse, the train resumes its rural progress, heading due north across the fields towards Wroxham.

THE line drops steadily from Salhouse to Wroxham, on the approach to which it passes the premises of Wroxham Town FC, founded as long ago as 1892 and nicknamed, appropriately enough, 'The Yachtsmen'. Long synonymous with Broadland boating holidays, Wroxham considers itself the 'capital' of the Broads, justly so when one remembers that this was where pleasure boating began, not entirely coincidentally around the time of the railway's arrival. Disingenuously, the station has, in recent years, gone by the name of HOVETON & WROXHAM in deference to the larger of twin villages on either bank of the Bure. But back in the 1930s when the Callum children and their new friend alighted from their train - surreptitiously in Tom's case, sensing that there would be a row over his unorthodox boarding of the train back at Norwich - the station was still plain Wroxham. Fortunately Tom was on good terms with the station-master, and the incident was soon forgotten amidst a round of introductions and local gossip.

'Never in their lives had Dick and Dorothea seen so many boats.' So began Chapter II of *Coot Club*, though it may well be the case that Wroxham's waterside is even busier with craft now. From the train you only catch a brief but bewildering glimpse of the river, but it's enough to make you yearn to detrain and explore and, if nothing else, at least arrange the hire of a day boat for a few hours. Downstream lies Wroxham Broad, over a hundred acres of surface water, likely to have originated, like most of the Broadland lakes, by the flooding of medieval peat workings. Upstream there's another four miles of navigable river as far as Coltishall. In the past boats could reach Aylsham. Nowadays the best way of reaching that picturesque town is aboard the Bure Valley Railway, a privately operated narrow gauge line laid along the trackbed of a standard gauge branch which ran between Wroxham and County School on the Wymondham to Wells-on-Sea line.

North of Hoveton & Wroxham the tracks of the Bittern Line have been singled. Briefly the standard and narrow gauge tracks share a cutting, evoking *Alice in Wonderland* comparisons in stature. With gradients characteristically switchbacking, the railway climbs once again in the direction of North Walsham. Level crossings proliferate, some now automated, others retaining their traditional timber gates, and being overlooked by charming wooden chalet-style keeper's cottages. Norfolk is well known for the quality and quantity

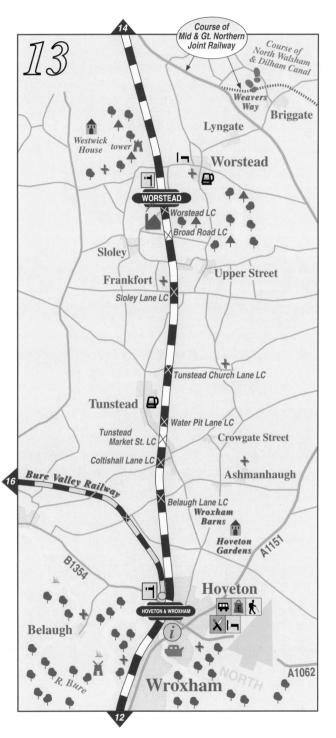

of its churches and they are in abundance hereabouts, scarcely at any point does the carriage window fail to frame an enchanting vista of traditionally hedged fields, small plantations of Scots Pine, and church towers in the middle distance. Many of the churches are isolated now, reflecting the former presence of lost villages, settlements which never recovered from the demise of Norfolk's phenomenal wool trade after the Middle Ages. St Mary's at Tunstead lies a good mile from the present day centre of the village, to the east of the railway. Out of context it seems massive. Closer to the line than most, St Bartholomews' at Sloley stands aloof from its village, as if distancing itself from the sin-prone frailties of mankind. The novelist, Sylvia Warner Townsend, lived at Frankfort Manor for a short period of time in the Thirties until she and her lover, Valentine Ackland, were driven out of the neighbourhood by gossip intolerant of two females cohabiting.

At WORSTEAD you can see where the line was once double, the old down platform, which held the main buildings, being trackless now. The signal box remains intact, used as a potting shed for many years. A road haulage contractor occupies the site of Worstead goods yard. Down the lane in the direction of Sloley lies Westwick Works, where Heinz process frozen foods; many of the workforce using the trains. Pulling away from Worstead, the village's imposing parish church is to be seen to the east, whilst to the west a curious observation tower, in the grounds of Westwick House can just been made out. Now almost overtaken in height by surrounding trees, it once boasted a lighthouse-like room at the top, octagonally-shaped with windows offering views in all directions.

Where the Wroxham-County School was fortunate enough to reinvent itself as a narrow gauge tourist line, the fondly remembered Midland & Great Northern south of North Walsham was fated to become a road. It swings reproachfully in from the south-east, concealed in a shallow yet still railway-like cutting, above the waving grasses of which you half hope to see the smoke trail of the 9.02 ex Yarmouth (Beach) with through coaches for Leicester (London Road) and Birmingham (New Street). This part of the M&GN - fondly disparaged amongst admirers as the 'Muddle & Go Nowhere' - disappeared, along with the bulk of the independent little railway's 182 route miles - in 1959, but at least its trackbed has been adapted as the Weavers Way public footpath, whilst you will encounter it again on this journey still in use as a railway.

THE majority of north and southbound (or down and up in the railway vernacular) *Bitterm Line* passenger services take the opportunity provided by its loop to pass at NORTH WALSHAM, the largest intermediate town on the line. There are other train movements as well, for gas is conveyed in tank wagons on a daily basis from here to Harwich by rail, bringing the welcome variety of freight to the line, a feature regrettably absent from most rural branches nowadays. Usually, around lunchtime on weekdays, a GBRF General Motors Class 66 locomotive will be lurking in the sidings to the east of the line, impatient to assemble the southbound, loaded train and get on its way.

North Walsham once boasted two stations, virtually side by side. The one in use today was known as North Walsham 'Main', its near neighbour, which belonged to the Midland & Great Northern route between Melton Constable and Yarmouth, North Walsham 'Town'. The town's by-pass has swallowed up most traces of the latter station. The railway historian H. P. White wrote evocatively of a journey made in 1958 over the M&GN from Peterborough to Yarmouth in *BackTrack* magazine (Vol 6, No.2) which includes a photograph of his train curving into North Walsham Town taken from one of its rear windows. From North Walsham he continued across the Broads through Stalham and Potter Heigham, eventually reaching Yarmouth almost four and a half hours after departing from Peterborough; a hundred and ten miles covered at an average speed of twenty-five miles an hour. Nowadays, conveniently but perhaps less romantically, fast diesel units cover the journey in around two and a half hours, though this does require a change at Norwich.

For a number of years North Walsham boasted a third railway route, the Norfolk & Suffolk Joint line to Mundesley, which continued round the coast to Cromer. The Mundesley section closed in 1964, the Cromer extension having succumbed in 1953, taking with it the mellifluously named stations of Trimingham and Overstrand. The N&SJ resulted from a sensible pooling of resources between the rival Great Eastern and Midland & Great Northern companies, mutually keen to milk the holiday-making potential of the North-East Norfolk coastline. Mundesley was reached in 1898, Cromer eight years later. Mundesley took off in a small way, Trimingham and Overstrand barely at all. Struggling to come up with good reasons to tempt rail travellers into gracing

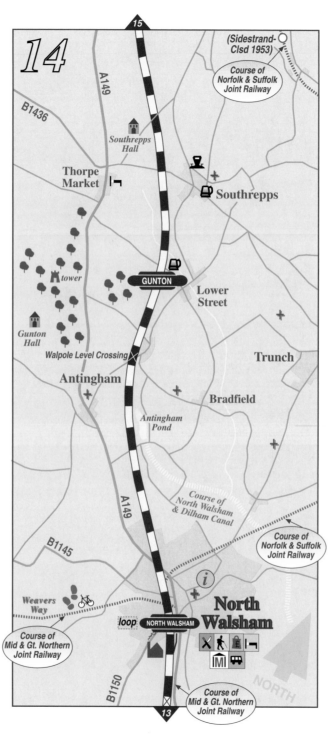

Mundesley with their presence, British Railways Eastern England Holiday Guide for 1952, wrote vaguely of 'firm sands' and a 'nine-hole golf course'; 'peaceful' and 'restful' being qualifying euphemisms for boring and tedious beyond description. The die was being cast, the Costa Brava looming on the horizon as a tempting alternative. In the good old days, however, the line flourished briefly, through carriages off the *Norfolk Coast Express* being detached at North Walsham to serve the optimistic hoteliers of an ultimately neglected trio of resorts. Not without irony, the trackbed between Mundesley and North Walsham was subsequently used to bury the gas pipeline from Bacton to the railhead at North Walsham.

Oblivious to the purple past, your train pulls downhill out of North Walsham on an embankment which carries it above the bungalowed northern periphery of the town. As it gathers speed you might just be able to make out the course of the M&GN westwards towards Aylsham, now enjoying a new lease of life as a public footpath and cycle route, part of the Weavers Way. A sequence of cuttings ensues, the span of occasional overbridges revealing that the railway's builders may once have harboured notions of doubling the track throughout.

Paralleling the railway are the upper reaches of the long abandoned North Walsham & Dilham Canal, a navigable extension of the River Ant opened in 1826. Antingham Pond was the northernmost limit of navigation. Twenty ton wherries carried cabbages from here for sale at Yarmouth market. A hoped for trade in coal didn't materialise, largely because it was cheaper and less time-consuming to land it from coastal vessels on nearby beaches and convey it by horse and cart inland. Barely profitable, the nine mile canal was abandoned by degrees between 1893 and 1934, a footnote in the annals of Britain's inland waterways.

After a section of level track the railway climbs towards Gunton with views of Bradfield's lost and lonely church to the east. Though out in the wilds, GUNTON station gained significance by virtue of its associations with Lord Suffield of Gunton Hall, a cohort of and frequent host to the Prince of Wales before he became King Edward VII. The station building, occupying the abandoned Down platform, has been beautifully restored as a private home. Note the little wooden train waiting to whisk you away on a branch line connection to Never Never Land.

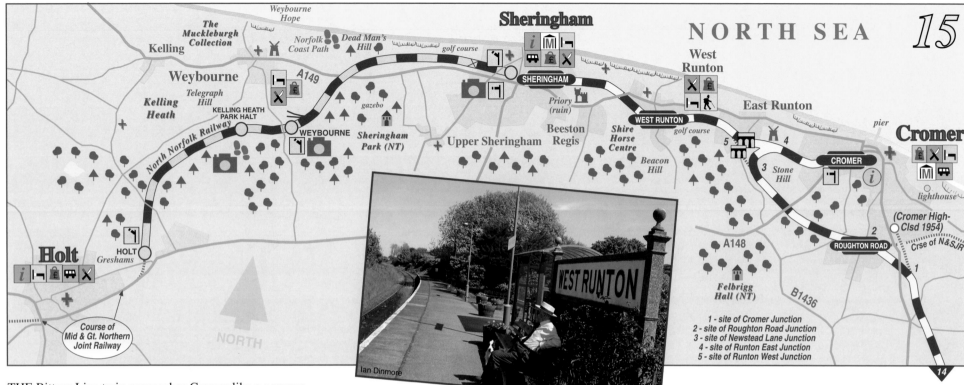

The Muckleburgh Collection
Kelling
Weybourne Hope
Norfolk Coast Path
Dead Man's Hill
golf course
Sheringham
SHERINGHAM
West Runton
WEST RUNTON
East Runton
pier
Cromer
Weybourne
A149
Telegraph Hill
Kelling Heath
KELLING HEATH PARK HALT
North Norfolk Railway
WEYBOURNE
gazebo
Sheringham Park (NT)
Upper Sheringham
Priory (ruin)
Beeston Regis
Shire Horse Centre
Beacon Hill
golf course
5 4
3 Stone Hill
CROMER
lighthouse
(Cromer High - Clsd 1954)
ROUGHTON ROAD
Crse of N&SJR
2
1
Kelling Heath
Holt
HOLT Greshams
Course of Mid & Gt. Northern Joint Railway
NORTH
A148
Felbrigg Hall (NT)
B1436

1 - site of Cromer Junction
2 - site of Roughton Road Junction
3 - site of Newstead Lane Junction
4 - site of Runton East Junction
5 - site of Runton West Junction

WEST RUNTON

Ian Dinmore

THE Bittern Line train approaches Cromer like a nervous fan seeking a celebrity's autograph, sidling circuitously up to its quarry, in consideration of the lie of the land rather than any inherent sense of inferiority. There are rational historical explanations for this. As first built, in 1877, the line terminated at a station well-advisably known as Cromer High, a mile from the town centre and two hundred feet above sea level. But our Victorian and Edwardian forebears were made of sterner stuff than the mollycoddled motorists of today, and this remained the end of the line until 1954, when it was abandoned in favour of Cromer Beach, a much more user-friendly station in modern parlance, opened by the Eastern & Midlands Railway - a constituent of the Midland & Great Northern - in 1887.

Pre-Beeching rationalisations rendered Cromer High superfluous, especially following extra capacity made available with the withdrawal of passenger services over the Norfolk & Suffolk Joint line to Mundesley in 1952. Whilst imposing and well equipped, no one would deny - not even

the railway authorities - that Cromer High was out on a limb, whereas Cromer Beach was much better situated in respect of the resort's hotels and facilities. The sadness is that Cromer's status as a premier seaside resort was already irreversibly on the ebb when the decision was made to focus services on a single station. For something of an Indian Summer the London expresses continued to run to Cromer and Sheringham, more expediently now that, in the down direction Sheringham portions didn't have to shed their carriages at Cromer Junction or, in the up direction reverse half a mile in an ungainly and virtually unique manner backwards into Cromer High. But their days were numbered, betrayed by dwindling passenger counts, and eventually the guts were ripped out of Cromer's railway infrastructure, leaving present day trains with the simple chore of reversal at a station now simply known as Cromer, the sobriquet 'Beach' a forgotten addendum, remembered solely by railway buffs of a certain age and temperament.

Gorse-filled earthworks are all that remain of the old line into Cromer High as your train veers sharply away to the left, negotiating a 'chord' laid down in 1906 to facilitate through running between the Great Eastern and Midland & Great Northern systems. ROUGHTON ROAD station dates from as recently as 1985 and was provided to serve Cromer's burgeoning southern outskirts. Sloping under the skirts of Stone Hill with wheels squealing at the sharpness of the curves, the diesel unit encounters a series of lost junctions barely perceptible now. Old photographs reveal that the signal box at Roughton Road Junction resembled nothing so much as a garden gazebo of the most elegant kind with its hipped roof, vivacious barge boards and disproportionately deep eaves. It oversaw the egress of the Norfolk & Suffolk Joint line, heading east to pass beneath the approach to Cromer High in what was famously Norfolk's only railway tunnel. Beyond the tunnel (all 62 yards of it) cuttings led to Cromer Links Halt, a handsome perk for golfers by all accounts

eschewed.

'Oh look, there's the sea!' Whose inner child does not experience a surge of excitement at that sudden visual revelation and the memories inevitably evoked of childhood holidays? You've breasted the ridge that runs from Holt to Cromer - giving lie to Norfolk's reputation for being largely flat, its own mini range of hills rising to over three hundred feet. Now, gingerly, on a curving, descending trajectory the train eases past the site of Newstead Lane Junction from which another chord was laid in 1906, south to west, to facilitate through running to and from Sheringham. Two unconnected tracks run parallel into Cromer where the much rationalised track layout consists solely of a pair of crossovers, there no longer being any run-round facility for locomotive hauled trains. Where the two tracks draw alongside each other there used to be pointwork and a junction known as Runton East.

A cutting swallows up sea views as the train descends into CROMER station. Clattering over the crossovers you come to a stand at one or other of the island platform's pair of faces. The once substantial yard, with sidings for goods traffic, an engine shed and a turntable, has vanished beneath a supermarket. Of equal length now, the northernmost platform once continued through a train-shed supported by the rear of the station building. The latter remains largely intact, housing a bar and restaurant known as Buffers. Viewed from the railway side it lacks character, seen from the road it positively oozes it, echoing the Arts & Crafts Movement with its mock timbering and diagonal courses of brick.

Not quite as close to the sands as its old name implied, Cromer Beach was nevertheless a good deal closer to the front than its erstwhile rival. With just two platforms it must, at times, have had its work cut out to cope with all the traffic on offer. Towards the end of the 19th century Cromer and its coastal hinterland was riding on the crest of a publicity wave resulting from a colourful travel piece in the *Daily Telegraph* by the drama critic Clement Scott. Big hotels were being erected, both to cater for and encourage, growing numbers of visitors. In the years leading up to the First World War, Cromer was one of the most popular seaside resorts in the country, and the railways played a key role in promoting and sustaining this status.

Once the driver and guard have swapped ends, the train reverses out of the station. Fine coastal views are to be had from the right hand side of the Sheringham-bound train. It's difficult to resist trying to count the number of ships out at sea, be they making their way along the East Coast on the horizon, or nearer at hand on the shipping lanes into and out of the ports of The Wash. Travelling over the tracks of the Midland & Great Northern

Railway the *Bittern Line* train reaches the Runtons. The last piece in the local railway jigsaw was Runton West Junction at which point four tracks funnelled into one under the watchful eye of a busy signalbox. You might just catch a glimpse of the old viaduct which, until 1963, carried the chord to Newstead Lane Junction on the left hand side of the train, but soon you are slowing for WEST RUNTON, a simple wayside platform enhanced by some charming floral displays which retains a typical M&GN name board of concrete manufacture.

The Runtons & District Women's Institute are responsible for the high quality of the station's horticulture. They hold an annual tea party here to raise funds for their splendid endeavours. If you're surprised that such a diminutive halt was considered worth opening in the first place, look up the road to the neighbouring hotel, a substantial pile which must once have wooed holidaymakers off such halcyon trains as the *Norfolk Coast Express* and the *Eastern Belle*, a land cruise Pullman train operated by the LNER between the wars which reached Sheringham on a regular basis. Beyond the hotel lies Beeston Regis Heath and wooded Beacon Hill, a picturesque landscape saved for posterity by the National Trust.

Pulling away from its penultimate stop, the train passes beneath the coast road and runs alongside a cliff top camping and caravan site overlooked by Beeston Regis church, long threatened by erosion with the Tower of Babel like ignominy of a tumble into the sea. For years the authorities have erected costly sea defences to protect this vulnerable coastline, but new schools of thought are now suggesting that nature be allowed to take its course. Beeston Hill is already less elevated than previously, but for the moment retains its local allure as a fine vantage point from which to view both the sea and the countryside inland.

Allotments followed by rooftops hint at the approach of SHERINGHAM. The line doesn't so much end here as peter out at the humblest of platforms capable of handling little more than a 2-car diesel unit. Formerly the railway continued across Station Road to a substantial station opened by the Eastern & Midlands Railway in 1887 to serve a growing resort that had every intention of rivalling Cromer's success. But post-Beeching, and the abandoning in 1964 of the passenger service through to Melton Constable, British Rail deemed it an unnecessary luxury - the level-crossing proving a growing hazard and delay to increasing numbers of visitors who preferred to reach Sheringham by road - and ignominiously cut back the line to its present terminus.

Thankfully Sheringham's original station survived, and became headquarters of the budding North Norfolk Railway, who were intent on preserving the Midland & Great Northern route through to Holt. Their operation has proven so successful, and is now so well-established, that there is talk that the level crossing might well be reinstated to facilitate through running, though one imagines a good deal of bureaucracy might be encountered in the process. At any rate, for a good part of the year, it is eminently feasible to continue by rail beyond Sheringham, and the need to change trains is mitigated by the delightful thought that the North Norfolk Railway's 'transport of delight' will be either a heritage diesel or a fully fledged steam train.

The North Norfolk Railway

It is a happy turn of events that the five preserved miles of the North Norfolk Railway, or Poppy Line, continue to contribute as significantly towards the district's tourist economy as the Midland & Great Northern Railway did back in the late 19th and early 20th centuries. Few visitors to Sheringham now do not arrive either specifically to make a journey over the line, or fail to take the opportunity to do so when on holiday in the area. The railway's wide appeal is evident as soon as you enter Sheringham's lovingly restored station; it might be the mid-Fifties, and you might be reluctantly making your way back home to the East Midlands after the annual ritual of a fortnight on the sands. This illusion is particularly apt when the North Norfolk Railway's flagship locomotive, the B12 (built to a GER design by Beyer Peacock in Manchester in 1928), stands at the head of your train, for it is representative of the motive power that worked in the area. Another appropriate survivor is the Ivatt Mogul based on the Severn Valley Railway. It would be nice to see it reunited with the line at some point in the future. The great thing about Britain's hugely successful railway preservation movement is that you never say never. Strolling out on to the platform you are struck by just how *pretty* Sheringham station is, its pavilion-like refreshment room colourfully painted cream and green, a colour scheme echoed by the glazed canopy's valencing. In its working days an equally substantial set of buildings stood on the opposite platform but these were demolished in the 1960s. In the early years of the 20th century the Great Eastern Railway gained a toe-hold on the station and a staff room was provided for them on the main platform. Nostalgically, it remains intact, used by the NNR as an office.

Find a seat on the train and settle down to enjoy the journey to Weybourne or Holt. The full ride may only take twenty minutes but there is much to see along the way. Departing trains move slowly out of the station so that the token for the single line ahead can be collected from the signalman at Sheringham's West Box. There was a box here in the past, but the one in use today originally stood at Wensum Junction in Norwich. If you're being hauled by steam it is nice to watch the smoke rings drifting back across the greens and fairways of Sheringham Golf Course as the train begins to pick up speed.

By Milepost 42 (measured from South Lynn) the line starts to climb before briefly levelling out then falling again as it skirts Dead Man's Hill, reputedly the burial place of victims of the plague. Inland you catch glimpses of Sheringham Park, a National Trust property dating from the early 19th century. The grounds are open to the public but the hall is privately occupied. A gazebo (opened by Prince Charles in 1988) affords extensive views over this ravishing coast and countryside, rightly recognised officially as an Area of Outstanding Beauty. The line veers away, crosses the A149 coast road, and begins a steep climb of 1 in 80 towards Weybourne. With your engine working hard, sink sybaritically back into the comfortable cushions of an elderly carriage and enjoy a retrospective style of railway travel. For all its high-tech glitz and glamour, modern rolling stock lacks a certain aura of 'personality' when compared with trains of the past. Incidentally, the former Prime Minister responsible for privatising the railways, John Major, has a house overlooking the line nearby.

All too soon you reach WEYBOURNE and its busy phalanx of sidings and buildings, home to the North Norfolk's fleet of rolling stock and motive power. Something's bound to catch your eye as the train slows. In addition to its stud of steam locomotives, the railway plays host to heritage diesels too: a Brush Type 2 (Class 31), English Electric Type 3 (Class 37) and Metro-Cammell multiple unit (Class 101) all appropriately reviving their East Anglian roots. One fascinating item of rolling stock at Weybourne is a former Wisbech & Upwell

Tramway carriage, a sister to the vehicle was used in the famous feature film *The Titfield Thunderbolt*, specially fitted out with a bar for the monied philanthropist (played by Stanley Holloway) who saved the line. Sadly the carriage used in the film was broken up, but the surviving carriage has been restored by the NNR, complete with replica bar! By most criteria, however, the rolling stock jewel in the railway's fine collection is their Gresley Quad-Art set of four articulated suburban carriages dating from the 1930s, currently under restoration funded by a substantial (and well deserved) sum of Heritage Lottery funding.

Should you experience a sense of *deja vu* as the train comes to a stand in Weybourne station, it does not necessarily mean that you've been here before. More likely you've seen this picturesque period piece on celluloid, for it is often - to the benefit of NNR coffers -

The NNR station at Sheringham

featured in film and television to lend chronological verisimilitude to costume dramas. Back in 1900 the M&GN lavishly erected more than just a wayside halt appropriate to the market potential of Weybourne village. They had their commercial eye on carrying custom to and from a palatial new hotel concomitantly being erected in the vicinity in the aspiration that Weybourne would develop into another Sheringham or Cromer. That hope was not fully realised, but a significant, if unforeseen, traffic - both in terms of men and materials - did develop here with the establishment of army camps at Weybourne during (and between) both world wars.

Whether you're proceeding to Holt or not, it's a nice idea to alight here and explore the station. The high-ceilinged Booking Hall displays some nostalgic photographs of the railway in its Edwardian heyday, but don't miss the charming Ladies Waiting Room and its M&GN fireplace. Incidentally, the NNR have licensed the station for civil weddings.

Weybourne retains its status as a passing place. The up platform on the south side is graced by a signal box and waiting room, both of timber construction. The signal box originally stood at Holt and was transported here by the preservationists because the original Weybourne box had been demolished by British Railways after the closure of the Sheringham to Melton Constable section in 1964. Similarly the waiting room, so the one you see today is a replica.

After the relief of a level section of track through the station, the line recommences its ruling gradient of 1 in 80. Passing beneath a handsome blue brick overbridge it singles. Look out on the landward side for the station garden with its air raid shelter, a delightfully subtle reminder of Weybourne's wartime activity. With woodland masking the view inland,

the eye is drawn towards the coast. And what a panorama! Prominent on the horizon, backed by a (hopefully) deep blue sea, are Weybourne's 15th century church and its 19th century windmill. The mill ceased trading around the time of the First World War. But it has been restored as a private residence, happily including its cap and sails.

Passing one of the characteristic M&GN 'summersault' signals, the line reaches KELLING HEATH PARK HALT. So steep is the gradient, only diesel railcars are permitted to call at this request stop in the westbound direction; heavier, locomotive-hauled trains might experience difficulties re-starting here. If you were to alight here, there are some fine walks to be had in the vicinity of Kelling Heath. Beyond the halt, the railway is enveloped in a deep cutting clothed by heather, gorse and bracken. At the far end of the cutting the line emerges into a heathland landscape at the summit of the line. An accommodation crossing proves useful access for walkers to the attractive countryside on either side of the railway. Curving southwards, the railway passes the site of Kelling Quarries from which the M&GN extracted considerable quantities of ballast and building materials. As originally surveyed, the intention was to take the railway down through the Glaven Valley to the small coastal port of Blakeney, and as such it would have swung away northwards at this point. In the event, the promises of greater riches at Sheringham and Cromer militated.

The original station at HOLT was handily placed for the town centre, but after closure in 1964, part of the trackbed was turned into a by-pass. The station where North Norfolk Railway trains terminate today is thus a totally new creation, though by judicious use of recycled materials and re-sited buildings the essence of a late-Victorian small town station is painstakingly being achieved. Nearby was Kelling Sanatorium which pioneered 'fresh air' treatments for tuberculosis early in the 20th century. Patients were housed in chalets erected on turntables so that they could be turned to face the prevailing breeze! Holt town centre lies a brisk twenty minute walk away past Thomas Gresham's prestigious school. Benjamin Britten and W.H. Auden were pupils here long before they collaborated on the famous documentary film *Night Mail*. The school's fortunes were transformed by the advent of the railway, the roll call increasing from fifty to two hundred because it became much easier for boarders to reach the school from other parts of the country. If the walk sounds too daunting on most operating days a horse-drawn omnibus connects with the trains, a suitably enchanting mode of transport with which to reach one of Norfolk's most enchanting market towns.

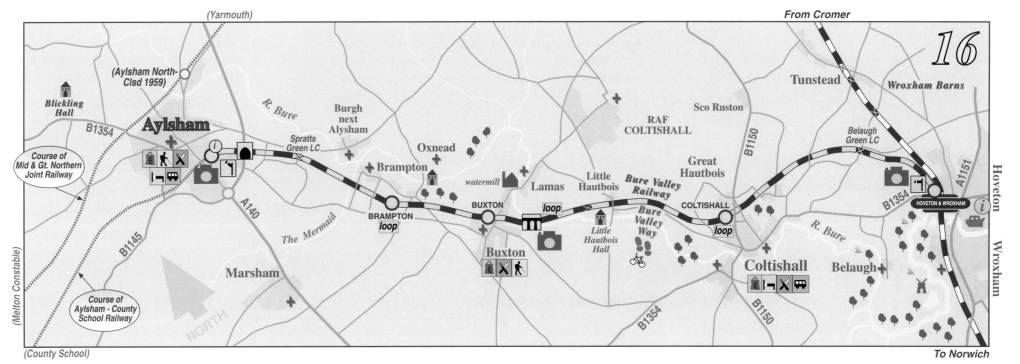

FEW modern Ordnance Survey maps fail to bear the frequent and melancholy legend 'dismantled railway'; or, even more dismissively, 'dismtd rly'. The majority of abandoned branch lines rapidly lost their integrity, being annexed by industry or agriculture, or simply reverting to nature. Some fortunate routes survived, re-inventing themselves as preserved steam railways or public rights of way. But the Bure Valley Railway is a textbook example of how old railway lines can be (and should more frequently have been) adapted for leisure use, being a rare example combining both.

Last used by goods trains in the early 1980s (mostly for the carriage of prefabricated concrete from a factory at Lenwade) the railway between Wroxham and Aylsham was purchased from British Rail's Property Board by the Broadland District Council in 1987 and leased to the Bure Valley Railway, or at least one side of its trackbed was, the other being reserved for the development of the Bure Valley Way. The new railway was constructed to a gauge of 15 inches and opened in 1990; the footpath and cycleway a year later.

The Bure Valley Railway's Wroxham station lies just

a couple of hundred yards or so from its Network Rail equivalent. Newly constructed in traditional railway style, it looks the part. Tickets and souvenirs are on sale here, though not refreshments. Incoming trains have to be run-round and their locomotives turned, an age old railway ritual which never loses its bystander appeal.

Ensconced in one of the BVR's comfortable covered carriages, departure is anticipated with rising excitement. Occasionally this coincides with a Cromer-bound train on the main line, and a brief race ensues. There is, however, only one real winner, and that is the snail-paced Bure Valley train, for what it lacks in speed, it more than makes up for with charm.

Going its separate way, the BVR veers west, plunging into a grassy cutting. The train gathers speed - or, at least, the illusion of it - developing a rolling gait as it emerges into an endearing landscape of patchwork fields, spinneys and hedgerows, before slowing to negotiate a level crossing at Belaugh Green; unguarded now, though still overlooked by the old keeper's cottage.

With the pleasantly nostalgic aroma of smoke lingering

in overhanging trees, the train proceeds to COLTISHALL through dappled cuttings, walkers waving happily back as you pass them by. The former station building remains intact, temptingly offering Bed & Breakfast. A passing loop has been provided here, and an island platform for prospective passengers.

The line skirts the perimeter of RAF Coltishall, one of East Anglia's premier military airfields, but one due for decommissioning in 2006. If this closure implies that the world's a safer place, then one must be grateful, though the corollary is sadness at the termination of such a rich tradition of flying, from the base's inception in 1940, and its association with Second World War flying aces such as Douglas Bader, Stanford Tuck and 'Cats Eyes' Cunningham, through to its involvement in recent times in hostilities in Kuwait and Kosovo. By all means admire those Jaguars as they roar off into the wide Norfolk skies, but remember that a little over sixty years ago they would have been Spitfires.

Conflicts come and conflicts go, but Little Hautbois ('Hobbis') Hall sleeps serenely on, a handsome, high-chimnied Elizabethan house dating from 1607; long enough

ago for it to regard the coming of the railway, its closure, and its reinstatement as so much dust on the table top of time.

The River Bure draws alongside, a narrow silver channel amongst watermeadows. So narrow that it is difficult to accept that wherries once traded up to Aylsham. Navigation upstream of Coltishall was abandoned in 1912 following flood damage to the locks, but by then the railway had plundered most of Aylsham's trade in any case. Another passing loop is encountered before the line crosses the Bure and enters BUXTON. In its earlier, standard gauge guise, the station here (whose buildings remain in domestic use) was called Buxton Lamas - Lamas being a pretty settlement on the far bank of the Bure, and the burial place of Anna Sewell, authoress of the children's classic *Black Beauty*. Buxton is a good place to leave the train for a walk in the neighbouring countryside.

Beyond Buxton, cuttings and embankments alternate, the latter offering grandstand views across the surrounding landscape. Charles II stayed at Oxnead in 1671, but most of the hall has been demolished, though the church remains. You could reach it from the wayside halt of BRAMPTON without expending too much energy. Perhaps it is a by-product of miniaturisation, but you can't help feeling an even closer resonance with the countryside through the carriage window than experienced on a full size train. Wildflowers which would pass you by in a blur when seen from a larger train, are suddenly revealed in all their individual shapes and colours.

The train crosses the Mermaid, a tributary of the Bure and presently the engine is whistling a warning on the approach to Spratts Green level crossing, overlooked by a tile-hung keeper's cottage. Then it's a downhill sprint to a tunnel beneath the Aylsham by-pass, and you experience an exaggerated sense of speed as the carriage lights come on and you shake, rattle and roll your way through the smoky bore, savouring those aromas which take you back to your misspent youth at platform ends.

Skirting the back gardens you reach AYLSHAM, an overall roofed station with all the gravitas of a small city terminus. And in high season, when the full timetable is in operation and a number of locomotives are standing around in steam, you might easily imagine yourself back at Norwich Thorpe in the 1950s, about to board a Britannia hauled express for Liverpool Street. The size of the splendid Bure Valley Railway is undoubtedly inversely proportioned to its impact

Gazetteer

Aylsham
Map 16

A sleepy market town living largely on its past glories - the Market Place being the jewel in its crown. Barclays Bank boasts a plaque commemorating Christopher Layer, a Jacobite supporter who visited the Young Pretender in Rome in 1721, before being arrested for treason and hanged at Tyburn two years later. The churchyard contains the grave and memorial of Humphry Repton, the landscape gardener responsible for the grounds of both nearby Blickling Hall and Sheringham Park.

Accommodation

AYLSHAM LODGE HOTEL - Norwich Road. Tel: 01263 734851 *www.aylshamlodge.com* Comfortable motel style accommodation about 5 minutes walk south of the BVR station.

Eating & Drinking

WHISTLESTOP RESTAURANT - Bure Valley Railway Station. Cafeteria catering for hungry travellers.

Shopping

Budgens and Somerfield supermarkets plus a number of quaint privately owned shops in and around the Market Place and Red Lion Street. Market on Mondays.

Things to Do

TOURIST INFORMATION - Bure Valley Railway Station. Tel: 01263 733903.
BURE VALLEY RAILWAY - Tel: 01263 733858. Nine miles of narrow gauge heaven - see text relating to Map 16.
BLICKLING HALL - one and a half miles north west of Aylsham on B1354. Fabulous National Trust property. Tel: 01263 738030. Self-catering cottages - Tel: 0870 4584422.

Walking & Cycling

MARRIOTT'S WAY - 21 miles of the former Midland & Great Northern Railway network re-invented for walkers, cyclists and horse riders between Aylsham and Norwich.
BURE VALLEY PATH - cycling and walking along the trackbed of the former Great Eastern Railway between Aylsham and Wroxham.

Connections

BUSES - Norfolk Green service X5 links Aylsham with Norwich, Norwich Airport, Cromer and Sheringham, hourly Mon-Sat and bi-hourly Suns. Broads Hopper connects Blickling Hall to Acle via Aylsham, Coltishall, Hoveton (rly sta) Wroxham, Salhouse, Woodbastick and South Walsham - carries bikes! Tel: 0870 608 2 608.
TAXIS - Jill Boast Cars. Tel: 01263 732727.
BIKE HIRE - Huff & Puff. Tel: 01263 732935.

Brampton
Map 16

Wayside halt on the BVR. Pleasant walks in the neighbourhood to the churches at Brampton itself, Oxnead and Burgh next Aylsham.

Buxton
Map 16

Bure-side village boasting impressive weatherboarded mill, formerly a restaurant but latterly converted into flats. A pub (called The Old Crown - Tel: 01603 279958), SPAR stores and fish & chip shop form the sum total of Buxton's commercial facilities.

Coltishall
Map 16

Sizeable riverside village with an above average quota of amenities. Nowadays this is the head of navigation on the Bure. Once it was a centre for wherry building - now you can only hope that it will cope manfully with the decommissioning of RAF Coltishall.

Accommodation

THE OLD RAILWAY STATION - Cosy bed & breakfast in Coltishall's former railway station overlooking the Bure Valley narrow gauge line. Tel: 01603 737069 *www.theoldrailwaystation.co.uk*
THE HEDGES - Tunstead Road. B&B accommodation close to the BVR. Tel: 01603 738361 *www.hedgesbandb.co.uk*

Eating & Drinking

RAILWAY TAVERN - Station Road. Tel: 01603 738316. CAMRA recommended village local specialising in Norfolk-brewed beers. Lunches.
KINGS HEAD - Wroxham Road (riverside location about 7 minutes walk from the BVR station). Tel: 01603 737426. AA recommended inn also offering accommodation.
NEW RISING SUN - Wroxham Road. Tel: 01603 737440. Well appointed pub on water's edge, bar and restaurant food, Woodforde's ales.
ANDAMAN ORCHID - Church Street. Tel: 01603 736655. Thai restaurant.
There are also fish & chip and Chinese take-away outlets in the village centre.

Shopping

Post office stores, butcher, pharmacy and LONDIS stores with cash machine; antiques as well.

Connections

BUSES - Broads Hopper connects Blickling Hall to Acle via Aylsham, Coltishall, Hoveton (rly sta) Wroxham, Salhouse, Woodbastick and South Walsham - carries bikes! Tel: 0870 608 2 608.
TAXIS - Caton's. Tel: 01603 737370.

Cromer
Map 15

The traditional seaside resort is alive and well and living (in semi-retirement) in Cromer. One trusts that a multi-million pound makeover currently under way won't entirely erase the benevolent ghosts of holidays past. Cromer doesn't need casinos to curry favour, it needs only tender care and maintenance to keep it in the soporific style to which it has become accustomed. Recall that Claud Hamilton, haughty Chairman of the Great Eastern Railway, on opening the pier in 1901 expressed the hope that Cromer would 'maintain its exclusiveness and cater only for those from the better paths of life'! The town's most famous son was Henry Blogg, the lifeboat hero.

Accommodation

CLIFTONVILLE HOTEL - Runton Road. Tel: 01263 512543. Imposing Edwardian throwback to Cromer's heyday. 2 Star hotel offering cliff-top views. *www.cliftonvillehotel.co.uk*
CAMBRIDGE HOUSE - East Cliff. Tel: 01263 512085. Exceedingly comfortable bed & breakfast overlooking the pier. *www.broadland.com/cambridgehouse*
CAPTAIN'S HOUSE - The Crescent. Tel: 01263 515434. Quality bed & breakfast with sea views. *www.captains-house.co.uk*

Eating & Drinking

TIDES - The Pier. Tel: 01263 512281. Cultured cafe on the landward side of the pier.
BOLTON'S BISTRO - Runton Road. Tel: 01263 512543. Part of the Cliftonville Hotel.
JACQUE - Garden Street. Tel: 01263 512149. Stylish restaurant open for lunch Wed-Sun and dinner daily ex Mons.
BUFFERS - railway station. Tel: 01263 514000. Carvery, bar and restaurant housed in illustrious premises of former M&GN 'Beach' station.
RED LION HOTEL - Brooke Street. Tel: 01263 512834. CAMRA recommended town centre pub offering food, Adnams and accommodation.

Shopping

Station yard now occupied by large MORRISONS supermarket where B17s and D16s once simmered between turns. Some good galleries, antique and gift shops in and around the town centre. JARROLD on Church Street have a fine selection of local books. Secreted away in alleyways you'll be able to nose out a number of fish merchants dealing in locally caught shellfish and eponymous crabs.

Things to Do

TOURIST INFORMATION - Prince of Wales Road. Tel: 01263 513613.
PAVILION THEATRE - Tel: 01263 512495. Famed for its long-running 'End of the Pier' seasonal variety show.
FELBRIGG HALL - Felbrigg (2 miles SW of Cromer). Tel: 01263 837444. 17th century mansion open to the public under the aegis of the National Trust. Paintings, library, orangery, dovecote, woodland and waterside walks, secondhand bookshop, shop and cafe. Self-catering cottages - Tel: 0870 4584422.

Connections

BUSES - links along the coast to Overstrand, Trimingham and Mundesley etc. Tel: 0870 608 2 608.
TAXIS - Blue Star - Tel: 01263 512645; Bernie's - Tel: 01263 513376.
BIKE HIRE - Knightriders. West Street. Tel: 01263 510039.

Gunton
Map 14

Built for the denizens of Gunton Hall, but now a useful railhead for the *hoi polloi* of Trunch and Southrepps. The water-powered sawmill in Gunton Park is occasionally open to the public - Tel: 01603 222705. The SUFFIELD ARMS is an extended and refurbished inn hard by the station - Tel: 01263 833461 - which has bikes for hire.

Holt
Map 15

One of East Anglia's most appealing small market towns, Holt's radiating network of quiet streets and alleyways encourage exploration and rarely disappoint. Many of the buildings are of Georgian origin and date from the town's rebirth following a particularly destructive fire in 1708. Sir John Gresham founded the eponymous school in 1555 when he was Lord Mayor of London, and it was administered by the fishmonger's Company.

Accommodation
THE FEATHERS HOTEL - Market Place. Tel: 01263 712318 *www.thefeathershotel.com* Homely, comfortable accommodation in the centre of town. Bar and restaurant food for non residents.

Eating & Drinking
BYFORDS - Shirehall Plain. Tel: 01263 711400. Exceptional cafe and delicatessen also offering 'posh' accommodation. One of the best reasons for visiting Holt.
RAILWAY TAVERN - Station Road. Tel: 01263 712283. Nearest pub to the NNR station with horse-bus connection.
OWL TEA ROOMS - White Lion Street. Tel: 01263 713232. Cosy tea rooms and bakery.

Shopping
BAKERS & LARNERS (Tel: 01263 712244) in the Market Place are the sort of 'old school' provisions merchants that most towns have sacrificed to the supermarkets, and to shop here is to recall a less frenetic age. There are other good food specialists as well - fishmongers such as FINNS on Bull Street, established as long ago as 1914. Holt also hosts some excellent craft shops, galleries, antique and antiquarian bookshops, and there's a specialist outlet for classical music called LUCIA POP - Tel: 01263 713031.

Things to Do
TOURIST INFORMATION - Market Place. Tel: 01263 713100.
NORTH NORFOLK RAILWAY - Tel: 01263 820800/820808 (Talking Timetable) *www.nnr.co.uk* Five precious miles of the former Midland & Great Northern Railway preserved in aspic - see text accompanying Map 15.

Connections
BUSES - useful links with Blakeney on the coast and Norwich to the south; you can even make a pilgrimage to Melton Constable, erstwhile hub of the M&GN system. Tel: 0870 608 2 608.
TAXIS - Stuart's. Tel: 01263 710088.
BIKE HIRE - Com-Trek Cycles. Tel: 01263 713293.

Hoveton
Map 13

See Wroxham opposite.

Kelling Heath Park
Map 15

Request stop on North Norfolk Railway at which only diesel hauled trains call when travelling towards Holt. Provides useful access for walkers to Kelling Heath and surrounding area. Bike Hire available locally from HUFF & PUFF - Tel: 07788 132909 or 01263 732935.

North Walsham
Map 14

North Walsham makes a fine base for exploring the lonely north-east coast and northern Broads. Over vigorous bell-ringing caused the steeple of St Nicholas to collapse at Ascensiontide, 1724 and it has remained romantically ruined ever since. As with Aylsham, the Market Place is the town's best feature, dominated at its foot by an unusual circular market cross. Nelson spent some time at school here at the Paston School, now a Sixth Form College.

Accommodation
BEECHWOOD HOTEL - Cromer Road. Tel: 01692 403231 *www.beechwood-hotel.co.uk* Award-winning Georgian hotel. Fine food locally sourced.
GREEN RIDGES - Cromer Road. AA recommended B&B in stylish 1930s house within easy reach of railway station. Tel: 01692 402448 *www.greenridges.com*

Eating & Drinking
PRINCE OF BENGAL - Mundesley Road. Tel: 01692 500119. Indian restaurant.
BUTTERFINGERS - Old Mitre Yard. Tel: 01692 500642. Cosy cafe for breakfasts, morning coffees, lunches and afternoon teas.

Shopping
The Thursday market has flourished since the 14th century. Elsewhere there are some solid individual retailers of character. On Aylsham Road the ANGEL BOOKSHOP deals in new and antiquarian titles.

Things to Do
TOURIST INFORMATION - Vicarage Street. Tel: 01692 407509.
NORFOLK MOTORCYCLE MUSEUM - Station Yard. Tel: 01692 406266. Splendid little museum devoted to the restoration and exhibition of vintage motorbikes and also die cast toys. Open daily from 10am to 4.30pm except for winter Sundays.
CAT POTTERY - Grammar School Road. Tel: 01692 402962. Cats and dogs pottery plus railway memorabilia. Closed Sundays.

Walking
Located on the Weavers Way, a 56 mile long distance walk linking Cromer with Great Yarmouth.

Connections
BUSES - Sanders service 736 provides hourly links Mon-Sat with various Broadland towns and villages such as Stalham, Hickling, Ludham, Potter Heigham and Great Yarmouth. You can also reach Mundesley and the coast by bus. Tel: 0870 608 2 608.
TAXIS - Victory Travel. Office manned 24 hours on station approach. Tel: 01692 405091.

Norwich
Map 12

See pages 21 & 22.

Roughton Road
Map 15

Halt handy for Cromer's southern suburbs.

Salhouse
Map 12

The village lies about a mile to the east, Salhouse Broad further still, yet there are footpaths which provide for pleasant walks and you can find refreshment at the BELL INN - Tel: 01603 721141. On a by-road off the B1140 (and within sight and sound of the railway) OLDFIELD provides accommodation and food - Tel: 01603 781080. The Broads Hopper bus connects Blickling Hall to Acle via Aylsham, Coltishall, Hoveton (rly sta) Wroxham, Salhouse, Woodbastick and South Walsham - carries bikes! Tel: 0870 608 2 608.

Sheringham
Map 15

Cromer's 'junior partner' in the business of providing fun and frolics on the North Norfolk Coast, Sheringham is a surprisingly small resort to have ever merited through carriages from London Liverpool Street. Once renowned for its fishing community - known as 'Shannocks' - its economy now relies predominently on retirement and tourism, and boasting a Blue Flag beach certainly helps.

Accommodation
BEAUMARIS HOTEL - South Street. Tel: 01263 822370. Comfortable 2 Star family run hotel just two or three minutes walk from the NNR station and less than 5 minutes from the Bittern Line terminus. *www.thebeaumarishotel.co.uk*
BAYLEAF GUEST HOUSE - St Peter's Road. Tel: 01263 823779. Friendly and inexpensive accommodation popular with NNR volunteers and just a hundred yards from their station.
TWO LIFEBOATS HOTEL - High Street. Tel: 01263 822401. Small hotel with sea views and restaurant open to non-residents.
SHERINGHAM YHA - Cremer's Drift. Tel: 0870 7706024.

Eating & Drinking
THE LOBSTER - High Street. Tel: 01263 822716. Vibrant town centre pub praised in the *Good Beer Guide*. Bar and restaurant food, Adnams and guest ales.
DAVE'S - Cooperative Street. Tel: 01263 823830. Fish bar and licensed restaurant which can trace its origins back to the 1920s. Eat in or take-away; also have a branch on High Street.
NUMBER 10 - Augusta Street. Tel: 01263 824400. Demure little restaurant, booking advisable.

Shopping
Gift shops predominate, as you might expect, but there are some good fishmongers (try the local lobsters) and butchers as well, one of the latter (on Church Street) rejoicing in the illustrious name of ICARUS HINES. Nearby is BERTRAM A. WATTS, an excellent stationers and bookseller; bookworms will also relish visiting the rambling secondhand bookshop on St Peter's Road adjacent to the NNR station.

Things to Do
TOURIST INFORMATION - Station Approach. Tel: 01263 824329.
NORTH NORFOLK RAILWAY - Tel: 01263 820800/820808 (Talking Timetable) *www.nnr.co.uk* Through tickets from 'one' stations.
SHERINGHAM MUSEUM - Station Road. Tel: 01263 821871. Open April to October Tue-Sun and Bank Holiday Mons. Local history : Shannocks, lifeboats and Zeppelins.

SHERINGHAM PARK - Upper Sheringham. Tel: 01263 823778. Splendid National Trust parkland designed in 1812 by Humphry Repton the great landscape gardener. Waymarked walks and viewing towers. Self-catering cottages - Tel: 0870 4584422.

Walking
Situated on the Norfolk Coast Path. Enjoyable woodland walks also to be had in the environs of Upper Sheringham.

Connections
TAXIS - Anglia Taxis. Tel: 01263 822222.
BUSES - sponsored by Norfolk County Council, the 'Coasthopper' bus service links Sheringham with Hunstanton and King's Lynn, serving en route Blakeney, Wells and Burnham Market, thus very usefully 'squaring the circle' in terms of local public transport. Sanders service No.44 provides a useful link inland with Holt, Melton Constable, Aylsham and Norwich. Tel: 0870 608 2 608.

West Runton   Map 15
Caravans and villas strung out along the coast road. Access via the village and Water Lane to a fine sandy beach, a rare gap between the crumbling ochre-coloured cliffs.

Accommodation
THE LINKS - Sandy Lane (a few hundred yards south of the station). Tel: 01263 838383. www.links-hotel.co.uk
DORMY HOUSE HOTEL - Cromer Road. Tel: 01263 837537 www.dormyhouse.net

Eating & Drinking
MIRABELLE - Station Road. Tel: 01263 837396. Restaurant/bistro just a couple of minutes walk from the station.
THE VILLAGE INN - Water Lane. Tel: 01263 838000. Well appointed pub offering a wide range of food.
PEPPERPOT RESTAURANT - Water Lane. Tel: 01263 837578. Cosy restaurant on road down to sea.

Shopping
Post office, SPAR and butchers grouped along the A149. Fresh crabs from CHAMBERS - Tel: 01263 861958.

Things to Do
NORFOLK SHIRE HORSE CENTRE - entrance adjacent station. Tel: 01263 837339 www.norfolk-shirehorse-centre.co.uk Fun for all the family, heavy horses working daily, indoor demonstrations on wet days. Museum, cafe and shop.

Walking
Good walks to the south along Beacon Hill and Roman Camp on land owned by the National Trust.

Connections
TAXIS - Pegasus Taxi. Tel: 01263 823546.

Weybourne   Map 15
The shingle beach at Weybourne Hope slopes so steeply that the deep water on its doorstep has long been perceived as a potential landing place for England's enemies. In the 16th century Weybourne was garrisoned against the Spanish; in the 20th century against the Germans, twice! Nowadays it is hugely popular with anglers who need protection solely from the cold.

Accommodation
THE MALTINGS - The Street. Tel: 01263 588731. Comfortable accommodation in handsome building dating back to the 16th century.

Eating & Drinking
THE SHIP - The Street. Tel: 01263 588721. CAMRA recommended village inn offering bar and restaurant food and a range of often locally brewed beers. Windows recall Steward & Patterson's brewery.
Light refreshments available at the NNR station and Muckleburgh Collection on operating days.

Shopping
Costcutter village stores.

Things to Do
MUCKLEBURGH COLLECTION - west end of village centre on A149 about 25 minutes walk from the NNR station. Tel: 01263 588210 www.muckleburgh.co.uk Military museum housed in former army camp. Tanks, artillery and missiles. Rides in personnel carriers. Restaurant and gift shop.

Connections
BUSES - the Coasthopper calls at Weybourne on its way along the delightful North Norfolk Coast offering every inducement to explore the area by stress-free public transport. Tel: 0870 608 2 608.

Worstead   Map 13
Medieval Flemish exiles introduced a smooth cloth here which still has currency throughout the world. In the 19th century production shifted to the powered looms of the Pennines, but in recent times it has been reintroduced to the village as a craft and there are even looms to be seen in the fine, high-towered church of St Mary's.

Accommodation
CHURCH VIEW HOUSE - Tel: 01692 536863. Bed & breakfast in the shadow of the mighty church.

Eating & Drinking
THE NEW INN - Tel: 01692 536296. Village centre inn about 10 minutes stroll east of the station.

Walking
Easy access to the Weavers Way at Bengate.

Wroxham   Map 13
If you can imagine Skegness, Rhyl or Ramsgate transposed in bricks and mortar beside the otherwise reedy banks of the River Bure, then you will go some way (but not all) towards cushioning the shock that Hoveton and Wroxham will inevitably wreak on your senses when first encountered. Flaunting their status as 'Capital of the Broads', they pander here to our basest instincts for fast food and frivolity, and very effectively they do it too!

Accommodation
HOTEL WROXHAM - The Bridge. Tel: 01603 782061 www.hotelwroxham.co.uk Modern riverside hotel with Waterside Terrace Bar & Restaurant open to non residents.
KING'S HEAD - Station Road. Tel: 01603 782429. Accommodation and restaurant/bar overlooking river. Carvery and home made pies.
COACH HOUSE - Norwich Road. Tel: 01603 784376 www.coachhousewroxham.co.uk Bed & breakfast in barn conversion.

Eating & Drinking
CANTON ORIENT - railway station. Tel: 01603 783939. Chinese restaurant housed in railway station.
KEN'S - Norwich Road. Tel: 01603 783739. Really good fish & chips to eat in or take out.
McDONALDS - surprising find in ROY'S food store! Tel: 01603 784397.

Shopping
ROY'S ('the world's largest village store') dominates, burgeoning to several branches including a Food Hall, Department Store, Garden Centre, Toy Shop and Boutique. Hardly surprisingly there are also a goodly number of gift shops to patronise.

Things to Do
TOURIST INFORMATION - Station Road. Tel: 01603 782281.
BURE VALLEY RAILWAY - Tel: 01263 733858. Nine miles of narrow gauge heaven - see text relating to Map 16.
WROXHAM BARNS - excellent craft complex two miles north of Wroxham centre on the Tunstead road. Childrens farm, gift shop and tea rooms. Tel: 01603 783762 www.wroxham-barns.co.uk
HOVETON HALL GARDENS - Tel: 01603 782798 www.hovetonhallgardens.co.uk Fifteen acres of ornamental and kitchen gardens in the grounds of Hoveton Hall located just over a mile north of Hoveton. Plant sales and tea rooms.

Getting Afloat
Numerous opportunities to acquire self-steer day boats, weekly hire craft, or enjoy a trip on a cruise boat. Here is a brief list of contacts:
BROADS TOURS - Tel: 01603 782207. Self-drive or cruise boats. Boat Train connections with the Bure Valley Railway.
FINEWAY - Tel: 01603 782309. All year day hire.
SHEERLINE - Tel: 01603 782527. Day and short-break hire.
BARNES BRINKCRAFT - Tel: 01603 782625. Canoe hire - equipment provided.

Walking & Cycling
BURE VALLEY PATH - 9 miles of traffic free walking and cycling beside the Bure Valley Railway.

Connections
BUSES - Broads Hopper connects Blickling Hall to Acle via Aylsham, Coltishall, Hoveton (rly sta) Wroxham, Salhouse, Woodbastick and South Walsham - carries bikes! Tel: 0870 608 2 608.
TAXIS - Wroxham Taxis. Tel: 01603 782925.
BIKE HIRE - Broadland Cycle Hire - Tel: 01603 783096.

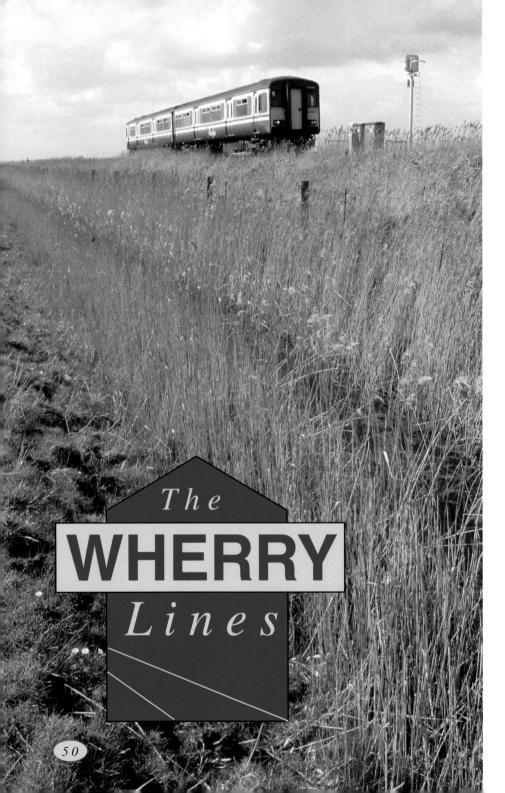

The WHERRY Lines

WHAT could be more iconic of the Norfolk Broads than the Wherry barges which once spread their huge single black sails so prolifically and successfully along the marshland waterways of this part of the world? An apt name, therefore, for the railway routes linking Norwich with Great Yarmouth and Lowestoft, and one which places you in an evocative frame of mind for a train ride to the coast across some of the most ethereal marshland landscapes imaginable.

The railway eastwards first forged its way out of Norwich in 1844, reaching Yarmouth via Reedham. Only a few trains use that route today, the majority travelling via Acle on a railway opened in 1883 to slightly shorten the distance and take pressure off an increasingly busy network. Out as far as Whitlingham Junction *Wherry Lines* services share a common route with *Bittern Line* trains bound to and from the North Norfolk Coast. But however many times you make the journey, it scarcely grows repetitive, each ride giving birth to new perspectives and insights.

The railway parallels the River Yare to the outskirts of the city. The largest vessels you are likely to see on this part of the river now are trip boats, so it can come as something of a surprise to learn that sea-going vessels traded commercially upstream to Norwich until the late 1980s. Coal was brought in by ship to Norwich Power Station until it closed in 1976. Trade thereafter was artificially prolonged because of high dock labour costs on the coast. It was even known for businesses in and around Yarmouth to send goods up to Norwich by ship and bring them back by road as a cost saving measure. Retrospectively, it is disappointing that the slightly surreal sight of a ship making its way judiciously up the winding waters of the Yare is no longer common currency.

Whitlingham lost its station in 1955. On the dark and rainy evening of September 10th, 1874, the up mail from Yarmouth was booked to cross a down express from London at Brundall, but the London train was running late. At this time trains over the line were controlled by telegraph. An ambivalent sequence of telegrams was exchanged between the night inspector at Norwich and the stationmaster at Brundall which resulted in both trains being despatched simultaneously over what was then solely a single line. They collided head on in the vicinity of Whitlingham, twenty-five people died and seventy-three were injured. Blame was divided between the Norwich inspector and a telegraph clerk who had sent a message without the mandatory authorizing signature.

Wherry Lines trains pass under the A47 on its high concrete stilts, before escaping into a misleadingly rolling landscape, hardly equating with the marshland you had anticipated. Postwick's Park & Ride interchange is a hugely successful innovation designed to take traffic out of the city centre. This is the old stamping-ground of Billy Bluelight, a Norwich eccentric who was in the habit of racing the river steamers. When he wasn't issuing challenges to the boats - and collecting pennies from an admiring public when he invariably won - Billy sold bunches of wild flowers in the summer months and cough sweets in the winter from his pitch by the Royal Arcade. A bench near Norwich station, on Riverside Road, commemorates Billy (aka William Cullum) and quotes his dates 1859-1949. He is also remembered by a popular pub of the same name on Hall Road, but wouldn't it be nice if his name adorned a train as well?

The rural illusion is as brief as it is disconcerting, by BRUNDALL GARDENS - formerly known as Surlingham Ferry - there are brackish pools laid with carpets of duckweed, reedbeds and bosky clumps of willow and alder which mask the returning river after its temporary desertion. To the south, hidden by woodland, lies Surlingham Broad, a notorious graveyard of sunken wherries, abandoned after their useful trading days had come to a precipitate end. The ornamental gardens at Brundall were a popular resort for daytrippers in the Edwardian era and after the First World War, and could

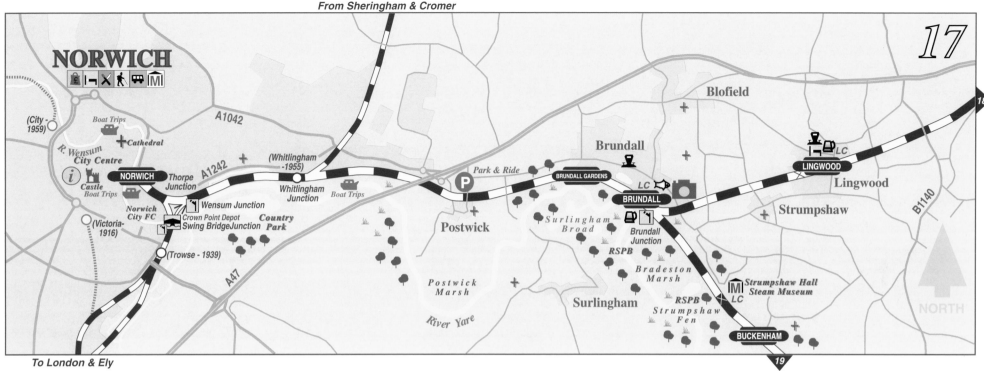

To London & Ely

be reached by train or river steamer. Thereafter they became a wilderness, though, like Cornwall's Lost Gardens of Heligan, they are painstakingly being restored to life.

Busy scenes of modern day boatyard activity intervene as you pull into BRUNDALL proper. John Sell Cotman's son, John Joseph, painted an Arcadian view of Station Road, Brundall, looking downhill towards the level crossing. For a time he lived at Thorpe and kept a boat on the river at Whitlingham. Broom's boatyard can trace its origins back to the late 19th century. Nowadays they build power boats and operate a hire fleet. On high spring tides salt water can flow as far upstream as Brundall. With its lattice footbridge, staggered platforms, well kept gardens and timber crossing gates (hand-operated by a resident keeper) Brundall station presents a pretty scene. Semaphore signalling adds to its appeal and, a short way east of the station, a traditional timber signal box overlooks the junction of the Yarmouth and Lowestoft lines.

The Lowestoft line heads in a south-easterly direction (passing close to the Royal Society for the Protection of Birds

reserve at Strumpshaw Fen) on its way down to the lonely, station at BUCKENHAM. Staffless now - and virtually trainless too - it featured atmospherically in the opening pages of *Black Sailed Traders*, Roy Clark's evocative book about the wherries in their working days (Putnam 1961). Roy, and his skipper, Jack Cates, alight at Buckenham at seven o'clock on a blustery March morning, give up their tickets and pass the time of day with the porter, then make down the track between alders and poplars to where *Albion* is moored under the admiring gaze of the village bobby. They had forty tons of logs bound for Beccles. Roy brews tea while Jack regales the policeman with river lore, expounding the tale of a wherry skipper who'd hung himself from his wherry's mast on the Buckenham Reach. 'Must have had plenty on his mind', remarked the policeman. 'Women or beer', rejoined the skipper, 'it's usually one or t'other'!

Meanwhile, from Brundall Junction, the single track Yarmouth line makes for LINGWOOD, a well-preserved station serving a commuter village. Bed & Breakfast is available in the station building, there are keeper-operated

level crossings on either side, and an old granary which once provided considerable traffic for the railway remains intact alongside the line. Anachronistically, a high-tech visual display screen nestles under a valanced canopy supported on cast iron spandrels bearing the initials GER. The Great Eastern Railway built Lingwood station in 1882. It only ever had one platform, but there was provision for a booking hall, waiting rooms, toilets for either sex and a house for the station master. All these facilities remained in daily use until the station was rendered 'staffless' in 1965. In the years which followed the buildings were bizarrely used as a doctor's surgery and a dress shop, but at least it survived and, for a number of years in the early 1990s the lady crossing keeper regularly won prizes for the quality of her flower beds. The crossing keepers are linked to the signal boxes at Brundall Junction and Acle and enjoy the use of their own frames for the pulling-off of distant signals either side of Lingwood. The mechanisms involved are thought to have no direct counterpart in Britain, though similar arrangements are to be found in India!

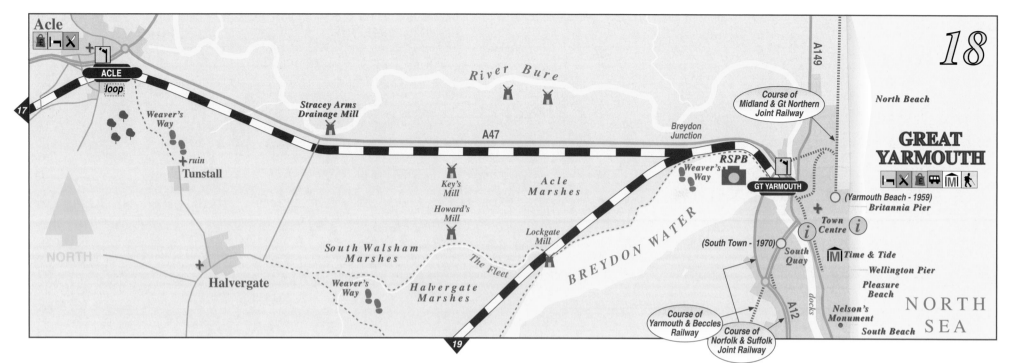

AS far as Acle the Yarmouth line slips undemonstratively through quiet farmland, alternately riding on embankments and penetrating grassy cuttings. ACLE station seems especially pretty on a wintry evening. Signal lamps glow red to green, and the frosty swish of signal wires is followed by an up train's horn echoing eerily over the marshes. Daylight reveals that the redbrick station building is of similar design to Lingwood. 'GER 1881' is emblazoned in the gables, suggesting that the building was erected a good two years before the trains ran. The booking hall and waiting room are available for self-catering hire. The goods shed, station master's house, footbridge and up side waiting room all remain intact and complete a timeless scene, and care is obviously extended on the flower beds. Henry Orbell, author of *Crossing Fences* (ISBN 0 9531659 3 0), was porter-signalman here in 1937. On market days, his book evocatively recalls, cattle trains of up to forty wagons were despatched, but the following morning it was his job to wash down the copiously slurried pens!

Singling again, as the landscape levels out, the railway draws alongside the A47 upon which a constant stream of traffic appears to move slowly in each direction, making you wonder why everyone in Norwich appears determined to drive to Yarmouth whilst everyone in Yarmouth seems bent on doing the reverse. The A47 is approaching the end of its journey from Birmingham, one of those useful cross country roads which have been largely by-passed in the motorway age.

The River Bure bends round close to the line overlooked by Stracey Arms Drainage Mill, a dominant landmark in the context of these marshlands. The mill dates from 1831, being built to aid drainage when the road was being built to Yarmouth. At one time there were eleven windmills downstream of Acle engaged in draining Halvergate Marshes. Stracey Arms Mill was in use for exactly a hundred years, worked since its inception by the same family. Replaced by an electric pump, it might well have deteriorated like so many of its cousins had it not been presented to Norfolk County Council for preservation. Fully restored to working order by the Norfolk Windmills Trust, the mill is now open to the general public daily throughout the summer months.

Having waved 'hello', the Bure twists away northwards again, its course towards Great Yarmouth marked by the stumps of abandoned drainage mills not so fortunate as Stracey Arms. The Bure rises in North Norfolk, close to the old railway centre of Melton Constable. It becomes navigable at Coltishall and is one of the most popular boating rivers on The Broads. On the skyline to the north there are distant villages backed by higher ground. Up until the First World War herds of cattle were swum across the Bure for summer grazing on the marshes. Prior to the Railway Age cattle would have been herded along the old drove roads for fattening in East Anglia. Daniel Defoe described cattle he saw grazing on Halvergate Marshes as being 'monstrously fat'.

Cattle still graze on Halvergate Marshes, you will see plenty of examples through the carriage window, but the landscape is to some extent artificially preserved. Common Agricultural Policies emanating from Brussels in the 1980s offered farmers financial inducement to plough these grazing lands and use them arably. It took intervention by the Broads Authority to retain the marshes in their present state. Landscape, like railways, rarely stands still. After all, up until the Middle Ages the land that the railway crosses was an estuarial mix of mud flats and salt marshes!

The railway comes upon Great Yarmouth in a manner reminiscent of the approach to Hull. It 'gathers to the surprise of a large town' in a way that has you mouthing Philip Larkin's poem *Here,* the one which opens *The Whitsun Weddings,* perhaps the greatest 'railway' poem of all time. The single track from Acle is joined by the original Yarmouth line from Reedham. Side by side, but unconnected, they skirt the top edge of Breydon Water on the last lap into GREAT YARMOUTH like two gnarled old wildfowlers comparing how many birds they've bagged. As the marshes retreat, the sky fills with roof lines punctuated by towers, cranes, monuments, chimneys and masts. Much the scene that would have greeted the twelve thousand eager excursionists on a convoy of no less than fifteen specials chartered by the brewers Bass one summer's day in 1893 to convey their workforce from Burton-on-Trent to Yarmouth for a seaside trip to remember.

By the end of Victoria's reign, Yarmouth had amassed three termini. Two of them no longer exist: Yarmouth Beach closed in 1959 along with the bulk of the Midland & Great Northern Railway; Yarmouth South Town closed in 1970, controversially severing the town's last rail link with its neighbour and bitter rival, Lowestoft, a dozen miles down the coast. Vanished too is the massive Breydon Viaduct which carried the Norfolk & Suffolk Joint line across the mouth of Breydon Water, its course adopted by the A12, the modern lift bridge a pale shadow of a substitute. In the course of railway history there have been four different ways of travelling between Yarmouth and Lowestoft - see if you can work them out!

Passing sad ranks of empty rusting carriage sidings - leftovers from the lost excursion trade and favoured now by skateboarders - the train curves sharply into Yarmouth 'Vauxhall', its four lengthy concrete platform faces more than adequate for today's operating demands. Damaged by bombing raids during the Second World War, the station was rebuilt in the early Sixties and evinces a curious retro charm in tune with the dwindling numbers of holidaymakers who still arrive by train. They face an intimidating hike to the seafront, no longer aided by boys prepared to carry luggage to their digs for a tanner. Overwhelmed by a surfeit of supermarkets and tarmacadam, the most expeditious approach to the town centre is by way of a rather shabby footpath, which passes the bow-strung girders of a former goods link with the fish quays, in crossing the mouth of the River Bure. This was the haunt of LNER J70 class 'tram' engines like the Reverend W. Awdry's *Toby.* One fears his trusty carriage *Henrietta* may have turned up her nose faced with such fishy smells!

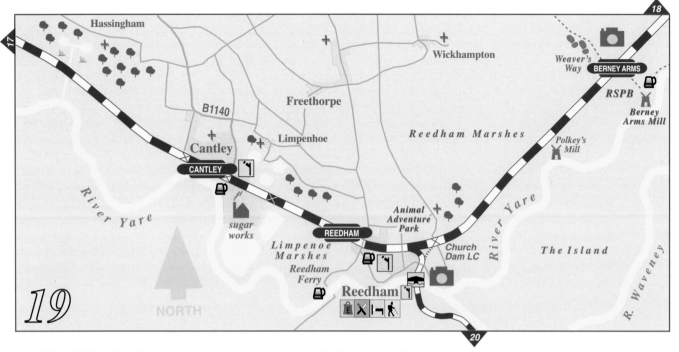

19

CLICKETY-CLACK, clickety-clack runs the train between Buckenham and Cantley, passing cattle grazing on the marshes under John Crome and John Sell Cotman skies. A reedy dyke runs up to the site of Hassingham Staithe. Wherries traded up this narrow arm until construction of the railway cut the dyke in half in 1843. Half hidden by trees, the isolated church of St Mary's at Hassingham has a round tower with an octagonal top.

CANTLEY station is fairly nondescript, but the traditional timber-gated level crossing at its eastern end is operated by the signalman, who springs purposefully down from his cabin to swing the gates prior to and following the passage of each train. The massive sugar factory dates from 1912. In the past it created traffic for both the river and the railway. Wherries sailed in with sugar beet from waterside farms throughout The Broads, and even from further afield, voyages from the Isle of Wight being recorded, though such distances didn't always bode well for the beet inside the hold. Sea-going vessels loaded sugar on their way downstream after discharging coal at Norwich. For many years the plant operated its own internal railway system, shunted by a pair of yellow liveried diesel shunting locomotives. Coal and limestone came in by train, sugar, pulp and molasses went out. Naturally, these days - unlike in Ireland - everything arrives and departs by road, blighting villages along the B1140 with a procession of heavy lorries, but at least consignments of limestone for use in the fluxing process are railed in to Norwich before completing the journey by road. Cantley Marshes support significant numbers of wading birds and wintering geese.

Running alongside Limpenhoe Marshes the train reaches REEDHAM. Here there is a plethora of pointwork and semaphore signalling and if the station environs are not as salubrious as they might be, draw consolation from the fact that the station remains popular with commuters. Furthermore, no truly thorough exploration of Broadland by rail can be considered entirely complete without a ride on the Reedham Ferry. Admittedly there's nothing much for the pedestrian to do on the far bank of the Yare - save for a mile long walk to the anagrammatic hamlet of Nogdam End - but ferries wear their hearts on their watery sleeves, and it would be a wasted opportunity were you not to sample this example while you have the chance. In the Middle Ages folk forded the river at Reedham, but reclamation of the marshes caused the river to deepen and a ferry has plied back

and forth since the 17th century. The present vessel dates from 1986, lengthier than its predecessor so as to cater for burgeoning sugar beet lorries. It claws its way across the water on chains, conveying two cars or one larger vehicle per passage. On occasions it pays to be patient!

At Reedham Junction the original line to Yarmouth veers away from the Lowestoft line, opened in 1847. Single track, it curves across Church Dam's hand-operated level crossing, passing within sight of Reedham Church - which was effectively burnt down in 1981, but which has been fully restored by determined parishoners - and embarks upon a ruler straight run across the marshes to Berney Arms. To form a solid base, the line was laid on a bed of faggots. Only two or three trains a day use this route now, but it's a line you should try to include in your itinerary, even if your schedule needs juggling to do so.

Two thousand acres of marshland, bounded by the Yare, the Waveney and the New Cut, comprise The Island. The marshes, made up of detached parishes, are employed for grazing cattle, rights being let in March each year at a pub in St Olaves. Grazing is confined to the summer months between April and October. More regarding this ethereal environment can be gleaned from a small, but fascinating book called *The Island Past & Present* (ISBN 0 9541683 1 3) by local author Sheila Hutchinson, who has also written *Berney Arms Remembered* (ISBN 0 9541683 2 1) and *The Halvergate Fleet Past & Present* (ISBN 0 9541683 0 5). All three titles are models of local history interpretation and can be thoroughly recommended to those wishing to learn more about the lives of the small communities which eked out a hard but also idyllic living on the marshes beside the *Wherry Lines*.

BERNEY ARMS - one of the most remote stations on Britain's railway network - is the stepping-off point for an earthly paradise of boundless horizons and reedy dykes. It owes its unlikely origins to the dogmatic insistence of the local landowner, Thomas Trench Berney, that the Yarmouth & Norwich Railway Company should 'build and maintain in perpetuity' a station alongside the inn of the same name which overlooks the vast expanse of Breydon Water.

The remote and tiny settlement at Berney Arms grew

around a farm called Five Mile House on account of the distance by water from Yarmouth. It seems unlikely now, but a cement works was established here in the 19th century, drawing some of the power for its machinery from a windmill which also drove circular saws engaged in the manufacture of herring barrels for the fishing trade at Yarmouth and Lowestoft. Two cottages, since demolished, provided accommodation for the workforce and the inn dispensed liquid and solid sustenance for the wherrymen whose barges traded to and fro upon Breydon Water.

When the cement works closed towards the end of the 19th century, Berney Arms Mill, the tallest on The Broads, was converted to a drainage mill, a task it fulfilled until after the Second World War when it was replaced by an electric pump. Now it belongs to English Heritage and is painstakingly being restored.

All the commercial activity of the past seems a far cry from the pervading sense of isolation which encompasses Berney Arms now. Old photographs reveal that there were railway cottages here, one of which doubled as a ticket office, waiting room, and post office. There was also a small, single-storey timber signal box, an intermediate block post brought into use during the summer months to provide extra capacity between Reedham and Breydon Junction. There is an especially evocative photograph in *Berney Arms Remembered* of milk churns being manhandled into the Guard's Van of a Metro-Cammell diesel multiple unit

in 1960. The few intrepid passengers who have enough sense of adventure to arrive by train can make their way to the inn when it's open during the summer months, go bird watching, or use the tiny halt as a staging post for exploration of the Weavers Way. Certainly they will treasure the experience of either alighting here, or flagging down a train to make good their escape back to civilisation. They should pay particular attention to the nameboard, made by a Limpenhoe boatyard from Singapore wood with gunmetal lettering. And if the rain has set in, or it's blowing a gale off the marshes, they can shelter in the tiny sentry box which passes for a waiting room (whilst doubling as a bird hide!) always assuming some fellow traveller has not squeezed snugly inside before them.

Between Berney Arms and the site of Breydon Junction the railway traverses further expanses of marshland, crossing Halvergate Fleet (Map 18), a saltwater creek before it was embanked towards the end of the 18th century as the marshes were being reclaimed. In 1884 seven drainage windmills lined the banks of The Fleet and a colony of marshmen operated the mills, maintained the dykes, tended cattle and supplemented their income by wildfowling. The windmills were rendered obsolete by the provision of an electric pump after the Second World War. The fortunes of the old windmills vary: Howard's Mill has been cosmetically restored; Lockgate Mill is a derelict shell adjoining the railway.

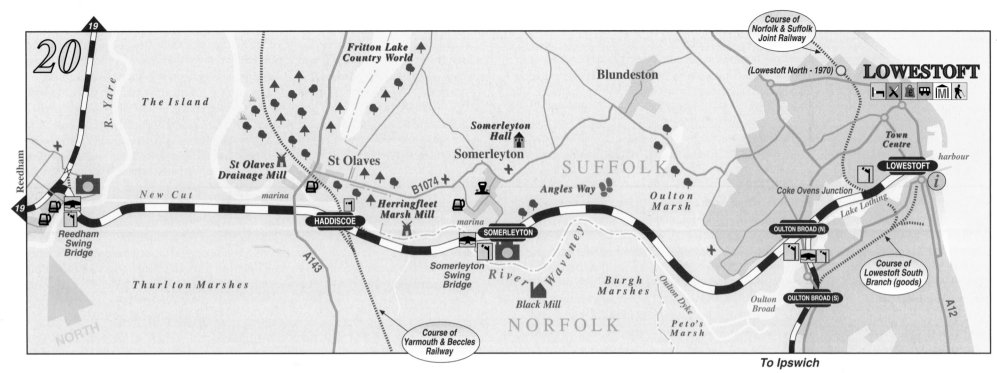

20

To Ipswich

LOWESTOFT bound trains leave Reedham on a sharp curve equipped with check rails. In the vicinity of Reedham Junction signal box there are still a number of telegraph poles remaining in use. From the left hand side of the train you catch a glimpse of the old south-to-east curve which facilitated the earliest through services between Lowestoft and Yarmouth. The curve was abandoned in 1872 when a new link at Haddiscoe was brought in to use.

It isn't only the riverbank reeds which whisper and rustle at Reedham, the swing-bridge displays its own sibilant qualities. So quietly does it turn, that you can look up from the pint you've been savouring in the beer garden of the Ship Inn with surprise that it has, unbeknown to you, manoeuvred itself into the open position for a boat to pass on the Yare. As a spectator sport the swing-bridge's movements leave little to be desired - the full opening and closing cycle takes around seven exciting minutes. On a summer's day it might have to open and shut up to twenty times. The smaller Broads hire craft can safely pass under it on all but the highest tides, but high-masted yachts and 'gin palaces' require more headroom. In the depths of winter

it might move only once or twice a day, yet the adjoining signal box is manned by three shifts throughout each twenty-four hours because of long-standing navigational rights on the river. In the past the signalmen lived in railway cottages on the east bank of the Yare, but these were demolished in the 1960s, and nowadays the cabin is reached via the bridge itself along a specially provided walkway on the up line.

The original, steam-operated swing bridge of 1846 carried a single track and was left open for river traffic when not required to be swung shut for the passage of a train. The present bridge dates from 1904 when the line was doubled. Apparently it cost just five and a half thousand pounds to build. The hydraulic pump currently in use dates from 1966. It was manufactured by a firm called Keelavite who went out of business a week or two after the pump had been installed. Fortunately it has proved so reliable as to require few spares! Sadly, as we went to press, a semaphore signal on the up line was due to be replaced by a colour light. But it had enjoyed a good innings, having more or less stood its ground since 1926 on a concrete post supplied by the Midland & Great Northern workshops at Melton Constable.

As the train rumbles tentatively across the swing bridge you catch a glimpse upstream of Reedham's attractive river front. Sanderson's boatyard and hire base has been in business since the 1920s, before that the site was occupied by the wherry builders Halls. Only two working wherries have survived into preservation. One of them, *Maud*, was built here in 1899. She traded for over a half a century but was eventually scuttled on Ranworth Broad. Happily, she was raised from her watery grave in 1981 and subsequently restored. Halls also constructed a number of pleasure wherries, notably *Solace* and *Hathor*, vessels based on the traditional wherry design but adapted for passenger carrying at a time when The Broads were being discovered by a new generation of holidaymakers. Fortunately, a good number of the such craft have survived - white-sailed in contrast to their black-sailed trading sisters, and are still to be seen on charter throughout The Broads.

Having crossed the river, the train completes an S curve, returning to the marshes and heading in a south-easterly direction, straight as a die towards Haddiscoe. It is fortunate to have a companion in this insubstantial landscape, the New

Cut, or Reedham-Haddiscoe canal, engineered by William Cubitt (a Norfolkman who went on to make his name in both canal and railway circles) in 1833 to shorten the distance by water between Lowestoft and Norwich. Concerns with silting at Lowestoft, together with the size of the debt taken on to build it, forced the New Cut into financial difficulty, and eventually it was acquired by railway interests. Following flood damage, the British Transport Commission attempted to close it in 1953, but leisure boating interests prevailed, and now owned by the Environment Agency (who have premises in what was formerly a manure and bone crushing works beside the line at Haddiscoe) it has recently been comprehensively dredged in order to play its part in flood control.

Nowadays the A143 Yarmouth-Beccles road crosses the railway and the New Cut via a high level, concrete bridge, but originally there was a level crossing and drawbridge here, the latter so rickety by the 1950s that buses were forced to disgorge their passengers and make them walk across the bridge while their vehicle followed cautiously over at a crawl. The bridge, which had to be laboriously cranked up from both sides, was the province of the railway signalman, whose remit was also to collect tolls from passing boaters, an exercise achieved with the aid of a long pole and a pouch.

The train reaches HADDISCOE, a lonely halt now in a marshland setting, but once a busy interchange with high and low level platforms and chords linking the two lines. Haddiscoe High Level was abandoned in 1959, along with the rest of the route between Beccles and Yarmouth South Town. So it is surprising to still see a signal box intact up on the higher level. And it is not until you do a 'double take' that you realise that it has been converted into domestic use in an enviable situation overlooking the River Waveney which the Yarmouth line used to cross by means of a swing bridge. The fondly remembered *Easterling* express used to storm through the high level station on its way between London and Yarmouth, more often than not with one of Sir Nigel Gresley's handsome B17 Sandringham locomotives at its head. R. S. Joby wrote evocatively of its journey from Beccles to South Town in *Forgotten Railways of East Anglia* (David & Charles 1977).

A row of railway employees cottages (still privileged with their own Royal Mail letter box) borders the low level's down platform, and should your train pause here, there's just time to make out the inscription LNER 1936 in the old concrete abutments which once supported

the upper line. Of the vanished chords it is interesting to learn that the east-to-north curve was used by passenger services until 1934 - as an alternative means of travelling from Lowestoft to Yarmouth - and that the south-to-west curve - a useful diversionary route for trains between Norwich and Ipswich - was used by sugar beet trains until 1965. Incidentally, one of the old Haddiscoe signal boxes has found a new lease of life in the unlikely setting of the Science Museum in Kensington.

With the surprise of a wooded escarpment to the north, and the continuing theme of low-lying marsh to the south, the railway parallels the River Waveney which forms the boundary between Norfolk and Suffolk. Windows on the left hand side of the train begin to fill with the agreeable view of Herringfleet Marsh Mill, the last timber-built drainage mill in existence. It dates from 1820, belongs to the Somerleyton Estate, is maintained by Suffolk County Council, and occasionally opens its doors to the public. Up on the ridge, Herringfleet's equally remote and equally interesting church pokes its rounded, Norman tower and thatched roof above the horizon. Somerleyton swing bridge carries the railway over the Waveney and in to Suffolk. Many august Victorian personages must have alighted at SOMERLEYTON station on their way to pay court to the local lord of the manor, Sir Samuel Morton Peto - 'Baptist, Contractor, Politician & Philanthropist', according to a plaque back on the concourse at Norwich - builder (of, amongst many things, the Houses of Parliament) and railway contractor who purchased the Elizabethan Somerleyton Hall in 1844, and promptly set about rebuilding it. Charles Dickens was a regular visitor, and the opening of David Copperfield is thought to be based on his experiences of the hall. Though shorn of its canopy, Somerleyton's station building remains well preserved and in domestic use, more imposing that one would expect of such a quiet, wayside halt on account of the Peto factor. Little remains of the local brickworks, purchased by Peto in 1849, though it created a good deal of traffic for the railway in its day.

With the Waveney now to the south of the line, your train continues its marshland odyssey. Most of the river's heavy holiday traffic in cabin cruisers remains hidden behind flood banks, but high-masted yachts make a picturesque, if surreal sight as their sails appear to glide in a disembodied manner across the grazing pastures. In time the river seems to tire of your company, twisting away upstream to Beccles, Bungay and beyond. The unusual late 18th century tower of the church at Burgh St Peter is visible on the Norfolk bank of the Waveney to the south-west. Boat captains use Oulton Dyke to reach Oulton Broad, and the railway briefly parallels this before deciding abruptly to turn due east and head for the coast.

The residential outskirts of Oulton come as an anti-climax after scintillating marshland vistas that you have enjoyed all the way from Brundall. Housing all but hides any view of Oulton Broad which you might have had. Maltings converted into flats overlook the railway. When they 'worked for their living' they belonged to the same company whose other maltings, further down the Suffolk coast at Snape, were converted into the well known concert hall, home of the Aldeburgh Festival. The station building at OULTON BROAD NORTH is occupied by a wood turner - Ladies Waiting Room' remains engraved on one of the windows. A handsome timber signal cabin overlooks the level crossing, whilst an adjacent public house recalls George Borrow's (he of *Wild Wales*, *Lavengro* and *Romany Rye*) association with the neighbourhood.

Beyond Oulton Broad North station the East Suffolk line comes in from the south, having crossed the head of Lake Lothing by way of a swing bridge. If views of Oulton Broad are denied the railway traveller, the same cannot be said of Lake Lothing, dockyard scenes prevail as the train rumbles over the last lap of its journey into Lowestoft. Until 1831, Lake Lothing was originally just that, an expanse of fresh water unconnected to the sea. Thereafter, by dint of a cut being dug through to the coast, it was extensively developed as a salt water harbour. Lowestoft's early 19th century attempts to become a successful port were not realised until Sir Samuel Morton Peto became involved, but under his galvanising guidance the town flourished, both as a working port and as a seaside resort. Within little more than half a century, Lowestoft's population had rocketed from two to eighty thousand. But Peto's success was shortlived. Cash flow remains the enemy of civil-engineering contractors to this day, and when the prestigious banking house of Overend & Guerney collapsed in 1866, it took Peto's business empire with it.

Though not as busy as in their heyday, Lowestoft's docklands still play host to a good deal of maritime activity: boat repair yards, facilities for the off-shore gas and oil industries, and container ships, all catch the eye. In railway terms, however, rationalisation has been more intense. The goods lines on the south bank of Lake Lothing, which once served various shipyards, a large Co-operative cannery and a timber works, were finally abandoned in 1972. But perhaps the most famous item of Lowestoft's railway infrastructure was the Sleeper Depot. Here, ready-cut railway sleepers, imported from Scandinavia, were unloaded then creosoted with the by-product of a nearby coking plant, before being carried by rail to many locations on the network. A narrow gauge railway was used to convey sleepers into the creosoting ovens.

In certain esoteric Lowestoft circles, 32C stood not, for the dimensions of a petite but not entirely unendowed size of brassiere, so much as the town's motive power depot. Classes of locomotive allocated here down the years included

Gresley Sandringhams and K3s, Holden's 2-4-2 and Thompson's 2-6-4 tanks and Sentinel shunters for the dockyard lines. The depot closed in 1960, East Anglia luxuriating in an arguably misplaced pride that it was one of the first regions of Britain to eradicate steam. In the evocative words of R. S. Grimley, compiler of the original *British Locomotive Shed Directory* the shed lay (as so often proved to be the case) at the end of a cinder path on the south side of the line at the junction of the Beccles and Yarmouth lines, 15 minutes walk west of the station.

It was from Coke Ovens Junction that the line to Yarmouth curved northwards. An extension of the Norfolk & Suffolk Joint Railway (a collaboration between those previously bitter rivals the Great East and Midland & Great Northern companies) opened in 1903, it provided a strategic interurban link between the busy ports and seaside resorts of Lowestoft and Yarmouth until being deemed obsolete to requirements in 1970; a decision today's tedious bus ride between the two towns suggests was short-sighted to say the least. Speaking of buses, generations of single and double-deck vehicles operating in municipalities throughout Britain had their bodywork manufactured at the nearby Eastern Counties Coachworks.

Another obvious casualty of Lowestoft's railway past is the fish traffic. Wilfred J. Wren, in his learned *Ports of the Eastern Counties* (Terence Dalton 1976) related that in the port's fishing and railway heyday before the First World War the Great Eastern Railway despatched a fish train of thirty to forty wagons every hour during the autumn herring season, even going as far as attaching additional vans to passenger trains as and when necessary. The Midland & Great Northern ran two or three trains every evening to the midlands and the north via Yarmouth. Lowestoft itself could not cope with the vast quantity of fish destined for export, and so trains were run to Harwich and Parkeston Quay for shipment to Hamburg, Rotterdam and the Hook of Holland. In 1909 the combined landings of herring at Lowestoft and Yarmouth totalled in excess of one *billion* fish. Additional traffic for the railways came in the caterwauling guise of the Scots fisher lassies annual migration down the east coast to clean and pack the catch.

The days when wagons left the harbour sidings dripping with fish juices are but a tribal memory. We like our fish frozen now, shrink-wrapped in cardboard boxes; a metaphor, for 21st century life as a whole. Rumbling into Britain's easternmost railway station (past the gregarious premises of the Sea Breeze Social Club) at the end of our exploration of the scenic railways of the Broads and Fens, one can only draw a line beneath the balance sheet of our 21st century imperfections in the pleasant realisation that, with railway travel, you journey not just through space, but through time as well. The buffer stop oil lamps, it transpires, are of LNER origin, whilst on the back wall of the station, facing the square outside, a fine dark blue Eastern Region enamel sign is emblazoned BRITISH RAILWAYS LOWESTOFT CENTRAL. Long may it remain there - the most easterly railway artefact in England...

Acle
Map 18

Peacefully residential now, Acle was in Saxon times a fishing village on the coast. Reclamation of marshland has brought it inland and now its watery activities are restricted to the passage of leisure boats on the Bure. Acle cattle market closed around twenty years ago. This was where Bernard Matthews, the 'bootiful' Turkey King, began his business empire.

Accommodation

KINGS HEAD INN - The Street. Tel: 01493 750204. Town centre inn offering accommodation and bar or restaurant meals. Menu features Cromer Crab and Marshman's Pie.
STATION COTTAGE - self catering. Tel: 01493 751136.

Eating & Drinking

HERMITAGE RESTAURANT - Old Road. Tel: 01493 750310. *Plus Chinese and fish & chips.*

Shopping

Co-op stores and Budgens supermarket. Barclays and Lloyds TSB banks. Small market on Thursdays.

Things to Do

STRACEY ARMS DRAINAGE MILL - Tel: 01603 222705. Imposing windmill located on the banks of the Bure approximately three miles east of Acle and prominent from the train. Open Easter to September daily. Tearoom and shop.

Walking

Easy access to the WEAVERS WAY a 59 mile footpath from Cromer to Great Yarmouth.

Connections

BUSES - useful links with Halvergate (for the marshes and Weavers Way) and with the coast at Winterton-on-Sea. Tel: 0870 608 2 608.
TAXIS - Acle Cars. Tel: 01493 750555.

Berney Arms
Map 19

The definitive wayside halt in the wilderness offering access to the WEAVERS WAY, Halvergate Marshes and Breydon Water. The BERNEY ARMS INN (Tel: 01493 700303) is a place of pilgrimage irrespective of how hungry and thirsty you are. BERNEY ARMS MILL is open April to September for pre-booked groups - Tel: 01493 857900. Access to RSPB reserve.

Brundall
Map 17

Bosky Norwich suburb given an added dimension by its location on the boat busy banks of the Yare. The station is riverside and echoes the industry of Broom's boatyard. Alongside stands THE YARE (Tel: 01603 713786) a popular pub offering bar or restaurant food washed down with Woodforde's ales. Accommodation is obtainable at BRAYDESTON HOUSE (Tel: 01603 713123) a Georgian country house in wooded grounds overlooking the river.

There's a fish & chip shop at the top of Station Road. Brundall station offers the best access to the RSPB reserve at Strumpshaw Fen whose visitor centre lies approximately two miles east - Tel: 01603 715191. Also nearby is STRUMPSHAW OLD HALL STEAM MUSEUM, a fine collection of steam powered machinery predominently from the worlds of agriculture and entertainment. Tel: 01603 714535 *www.steammuseum.com*

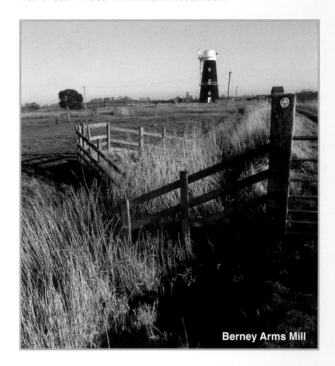
Berney Arms Mill

Buckenham
Map 17

With few trains condescending to call, it takes a determined traveller to avail themselves of Buckenham's lonely hinterland. Yet the octagonally towered church is worthy of investigation, there is access to riverbank paths along the Yare, and a country mile will take you to the RSPB reserve at Strumpshaw Fen.

Cantley
Map 19

Dormitory village in the shadow of British Sugar's huge riverside plant. Few facilities but a nice pub called THE REEDCUTTER (Tel: 01493 701099) just a short stroll down Station Road beside the raised floodbank of the Yare. It offers a good choice of food (including breakfast throughout the tourist season) and, belonging to the Reedham-based Humpty Dumpty brewery, features their excellent beers. Access from the station to a nearby RSPB reserve on Cantley Marshes.

Great Yarmouth
Map 18

If the front exudes all the vulgarity of a saucy Donald McGill postcard, there are other elements to Great Yarmouth's character which will appeal to the inquisitive visitor. The old market town core - which features the largest parish church in England - comes sandwiched between the seaside resort on one side and a working port on the other. In between one comes upon alleyways and backstreets of considerable charm, time capsuled leftovers from Yarmouth's lost prominence as a fishing port. Dog the Yare on its peculiarly reluctant journey to the sea and you will come upon many unexpected treasures: an 18th century Naval Hospital, a lofty column commemorating Nelson, a gas fired power station, and - eventually - an oddly downbeat and inevitably windswept assignation with the briny. Return via Marine Parade and you will have witnessed the comedy and tragedy of civilisation in equal measure.

Accommodation

STAR HOTEL - Hall Quay. Tel: 01493 842294. Half-timbered, balconied hotel overlooking the harbour and within easy reach of the station. Nice lounge.*www.elizabethhotels.co.uk*
HOTEL ELIZABETH - Marine Parade. Tel: 01493 855551. Three star sea front hotel.*www.elizabethhotels.co.uk*

Eating & Drinking

ST JOHN'S HEAD - North Quay. Tel: 01493 843443. CAMRA recommended real ale pub featuring Elgood's (of Wisbech) splendid ales plus many guest beers. Less than 5 minutes walk south from the station.
IVY'S NOTED TEA SHOP - Tel: 01493 855981. Dockland cafe urging you to 'stop here for a good cup of tea'!

Shopping

Regent Street will provide you with souvenirs a plenty to cram in your suitcase. In contrast, the Market Place is rewardingly authentic, being specially noted for a plethora of chip stalls reminiscent of Belgium and Flanders. Good secondhand bookshop called FERROWS on Howard Street South.

Things to Do

TOURIST INFORMATION - Town Hall (Tel: 01493 846347) or Central Marine Parade (Tel: 01493 842195) *www.great-yarmouth.co.uk*
TIME & TIDE - Blackfriars Road. Tel: 01493 745526. Brilliant new celebration of Yarmouth's seafaring heritage housed appropriately in a former herring curing factory.
GREAT YARMOUTH MUSEUMS - various locations. Tel: 01493 745526. Includes Row 111, the Old Merchants House, Greyfriars Cloisters, the Tolhouse Museum, Elizabethan House Museum, and Norfolk Nelson Museum.
MUSEUM OF HISTORIC SMOKE HOUSES & GT YARMOUTH POTTERY - Blackfriars Road. Tel: 01493 850585.

Walking

Gateway to the WEAVERS WAY, a 58 mile long distance footpath which winds its way through the northern Broads to Cromer on the North Norfolk coast.

continued on page 60

Connections
BUSES - coastwise services north and south form useful connections, especially with Lowestoft, a rail link irrationally abandoned in 1970. Tel: 0870 608 2 608.
TAXIS - Anglia Taxis. Tel: 01493 855855.

Haddiscoe   *Map 20*
The village lies two miles to the south by way of a busy road hardly conducive to pedestrians. Closer at hand is St Olaves where refreshment is obtainable either at the BELL INN (Tel: 01493 488249) or PRIORY FARM RESTAURANT (Tel: 01493 488432).

Lingwood   *Map 17*
Built-up village of inscrutable cul-de-sacs and closes. Homely B&B at the STATION HOUSE - Tel: 01603 715872 *www.stationhouseonline.com* Just along Station Road stands the KING'S HEAD, a congenial pub offering bar and restaurant food - Tel: 01603 713168.
Bus No.17A (Tel: 0870 608 2 608) provides convenient access to the RSPB reserve at Strumpshaw Fen - Tel: 01603 715191.

Lowestoft   *Map 20*
You emerge from the station directly into a maritime environment of harbour walls and ship's prows. And if the local postcards which proclaim Lowestoft both 'beautiful and Britain's most Easterly town' are only fifty per cent accurate, you are not disposed to quibble, because 'atmosphere' proves itself a more than adequate deputy for beauty. The town's most distinctive feature are its 'Scores' - precipitous alleyways which plunge down from the old High Street to the shoreline, the wayfares of fisherfolk in times gone by.
Accommodation
HOTEL HATFIELD - The Esplanade. Tel: 01502 565337. Best Western 3 star hotel with sea views. *www.elizabethhotels.co.uk*
Eating & Drinking
TRIANGLE TAVERN - St Peter's Street. Tel: 01502 582711. Home of the Green Jack Brewery, features in the *Good Beer Guide*.
GENEVA - High Street. Tel: 01502 580303. Cafe/deli.
CAFE RENAISSANCE - High Street. Tel: 01502 516377.
EAST POINT PAVILION RESTAURANT - Royal Plain. Conservatory cafe/restaurant overlooking the harbour and seafront within 2 minutes walk of the station. Tel: 01502 514402.
Shopping
The chain stores of London Road North stretch uphill from the station, before transforming themselves into the old curiosity shops of High Street. The BRITTEN CENTRE shopping precinct derives its name from the composer Benjamin, born in Lowestoft in 1913. RUSHMORE & OLDMAN, fish merchants, Battery Green Road - Tel: 01502 563617.
Things to Do
TOURIST INFORMATION - Royal Plain. Tel: 01502 533600.

MARITIME MUSEUM - Whapload Road. Tel: 01502 561963. The history of Lowestoft as a fishing port par excellence and its use in WWII by minesweepers and patrol boats aka 'Harry Tate's Navy'.
EAST ANGLIA TRANSPORT MUSEUM - Carlton Colville. Tel: 01502 518459 *www.eatm.org.uk* Make your way south from Lowestoft by bus or taxi and enjoy working trams, tolleybuses and a narrow gauge railway.
Walking
The ANGLES WAY will lead you north, the SUFFOLK COAST PATH in the opposite direction. More locally the TIC will provide you with leaflets to a number of themed trails in and around the town centre.
Connections
BUSES - useful links along the coast - north to Gorleston and Great Yarmouth, south to Southwold. Tel: 0870 608 2 608.
TAXIS - Atlas. Tel: 01502 500000. Five One - Tel: 01502 515151.
BIKE HIRE - Streetlife. Tel: 01502 585968.

Norwich   *Map 17*
See pages 21 & 22

Oulton Broad   *Map 20*
Busy Broadland boating centre where the River Waveney makes its way into Lake Lothing and the sea.
Eating, Drinking & Accommodation
WHERRY HOTEL - Bridge Road. Tel: 01502 516845. Ornate Edwardian hotel overlooking the entrance to Oulton Broad. Owned and operated by the Elizabeth Hotels group.
IVY HOUSE FARM HOTEL/THE CROOKED BARN - Beccles Road. Tel: 01502 501353. Three Star AA recommended accommodation on the southern edge of Oulton Broad. Fine dining in an 18th century thatched barn.
THE RED HERRING - Bridge Road. Tel: 01502 566499. Italian restaurant and wine bar.
Things to Do
River trips (Tel: 01502 574903) and self-drive boat hire (Tel: 012502 513087) from Oulton Broad Yacht Station adjoining the bascule bridge.
LOWESTOFT MUSEUM - Everitt Park. Tel: 01502 511457. Local history and Lowestoft Porcelain.

Reedham   *Map 19*
Snug riparian village lent additional colour by its railway swingbridge and chain ferry. A pleasant spot to saunter on a summer's day. A lengthier stroll will take you to the eastern outskirts of the village and the parish church of St John the Baptist. Effectively all but fully destroyed by fire in 1981, it has been faithfully restored with the determination of its parishoners. As work was taking place the remains of a Roman lighthouse were discovered, vividly recalling that Reedham was long ago a coastal settlement. New stained glass comprises a beautiful map of the village.

Accommodation
FUCHSIA COTTAGE - Riverside. Tel: 01493 701999. Bed & Breakfast.
THE PYGHTIE - The Hills. Tel: 01493 701262. Bed & Breakfast.
Eating & Drinking
THE RAILWAY TAVERN - Tel: 01493 700340. Congenial pub which has served rail travellers since 1844. Bar food, East Anglian beers and bed & breakfast.
REEDHAM FERRY INN - Tel: 01493 700429. Popular riverside inn offering bar and restaurant food about 10 minutes stroll from the station.
There are two other good pubs (The Lord Nelson and The Ship) on the riverbank close to the swing-bridge, and there's a small fish & chip shop (Tel: 01493 700706) in the centre of the village.
Shopping
Post Office on the riverfront near the swing-bridge. Small general store in village centre adjoining fish & chip shop.
Things to Do
PETTITTS ANIMAL ADVENTURE PARK - Church Road. Tel: 01493 700094 *www.pettittsadventurepark.co.uk* Entrance by the church, approximately a mile east of the station. Open daily April to October. Young family fun with the animals.
HUMPTY DUMPTY BREWERY - Church Road. Tel: 01493 701818 *www.humptydumptybrewery.com* Micro-brewery which informally offers visitors the opportunity to witness the brewing process and to purchase examples of their fine range of bottled beers, many of which (like the brewery itself) have East Anglian railway-themed names.
Connections
BUSES - links with Acle via Halvergate (for the Weavers Way) - Tel: 0870 608 2 608.
TAXIS - Tel: 01493 700146.

Somerleyton   *Map 20*
Charming estate village created by Samuel Morton Peto on acquiring the manor in 1844.
Eating & Drinking
DUKES HEAD - Tel: 01502 730281. Comfortable country inn (owned by the Somerleyton Estate) reached (in about 10 minutes) via the footpath which heads in a north-westerly direction from the station.
Shopping
Post office stores.
Things to Do
SOMERLEYTON HALL - Tel: 01502 730224 *www.somerleyton.co.uk* Extensive and imposing Victorian mansion, in the same family since Peto was forced to decamp so ignominiously in 1863. Yew maze in the grounds. Teas in the Winter Garden and gift Shop.
Walking
Access to the Angles Way which links Great Yarmouth with Lowestoft via Burgh Castle and Oulton Broad.

Information

Using This Guide

Twenty 'one inch to one mile' maps portray the course of the lines covered within. Each map is accompanied by a running commentary on matters historical, topographical and related to railway operation. At the end of each section a Gazetteer gives details of most of the places served by rail on each line. The Gazetteer gives a pithy 'pen portrait' of each place together (where appropriate) with lists of places to seek refreshment and find accommodation, details of shops and places to visit, tourist information, visitor centres, cycling, walking, and connecting forms of public transport. Where accuracy in such matters is essential, you are urged to contact the telephone number or website quoted for up to date details.

Scheduled Services

Three Train operating Companies currently provide services on the Network Rail routes covered by this guide. On the *Brecks Line* between Cambridge and Norwich trains are operated by 'one' Anglia. Additional services link Ely with Norwich and they are operated by Central Trains. On the *Fen Line* between Cambridge, Ely and King's Lynn most trains are operated by WAGN, with a few peak hour additions supplemented by 'one' Anglia. From Norwich, services on the *Bittern Line* and *Wherry Lines* are exclusively provided by 'one' Anglia. Virtually without exception, all the above services are provided by modern diesel and electric units of classes 365, 170 and 150 and 153, though in the latter two instances these are earmarked to be replaced by class 156 units. At the time of writing the 06.22 from Yarmouth to London and the 17.00 return are rostered for Class 47 traction to and from Norwich, though, frequently, the evening train in particular does not run between Norwich and Yarmouth because 'one' do not always have sufficient numbers of drivers passed on these classic machines to crew the train.

The Bure Valley and North Norfolk railways are privately operated. Narrow gauge steam locomotives provide the haulage on the former; standard gauge steam or diesel locomotives or diesel multiple units the latter.

Charter Trains

A number of charter train operators make it their business to visit East Anglia from time to time. Amongst these are:
Green Express - Tel: 01723 891400 www.greenexpressrailtours.me.uk
Past-Time Rail - Tel: 0871 871 4119 www.past-timerail.co.uk
Steamy Affairs - Tel: 01553 828107 www.steamyaffairs.net
Heartlands Rail - Tel: 0845 607 6 395 www.heartlandrail.com
In the opposite direction the following North Walsham based company operates a regular series of tours from stations in Norfolk and the neighbouring counties to many parts of the country.
NENTA Train Tours -Tel: 01692 406152 www.nentatraintours.co.uk

Bicycles

'one' carry bicycles on their services in specially designated areas for a flat fee of £1. Wagn carry them free of charge where capacity is available. Central Trains carry bicycles on their trains between Ely and Norwich but they must be booked for in advance - Tel: 0870 609 60 60.

Tickets & Travelcards

The stations at Cambridge, Ely, Thetford, Norwich, Downham Market, King's Lynn, Great Yarmouth and Lowestoft are staffed and have ticket offices - elsewhere, tickets must either be purchased in advance or obtained on the train. You might consider purchase of a travel card a good investment. Both the Bittern and Wherry lines offer Day Rover tickets, whilst the Anglia Plus card offers travel throughout the region at an extremely reasonable rate. 'one' has recently opened a Customer Service Centre based in Norwich offering a 'one-stop shop' for customer services and telesales - Tel: 0845 600 7245.

Useful Telephone Numbers

National Rail Enquiries - 08457 484950
North Norfolk Railway - 01263 820800
Bure Valley Railway - 01263 733858

Useful Websites

Rail Contacts
www.nationalrail.co.uk
www.onerailway.com
www.wagn.co.uk
www.centraltrains.co.uk
www.bitternline.com
www.wherrylines.org.uk
www.BritRail.net

Tourism Contacts
www.visiteastofengland.com
www.visitcambridge.org
www.brecks.org
www.visitwestnorfolk.com
www.visitnorwich-area.co.uk
www.north-norfolk.gov.uk
www.norfolkbroads.com

Other Organisations
www.rspb.org.uk
www.nationaltrust.org.uk
www.ctc.org.uk

The publishers are extremely grateful to the following organisations who have sponsored and encouraged publication of this guide.

Bittern Line Community Rail Partnership

The Bittern Line Community Rail Partnership was formed in 1996 after Norfolk County Council sought further development of local railways from Norwich. The aims of the Partnership are to encourage greater patronage and growth of the Sheringham to Norwich railway line. The Partnership is funded by North Norfolk Council, Broadland District Council, East of England Development Agency, the Association of Community Rail Partnerships, local parish councils, businesses along the route, Norfolk County Council and 'one' railway. Network Rail offer support and assistance where needed. The Partnership also works with the North Norfolk Railway (The Poppy Line), the Bure Valley Railway and the National Trust to promote rail access to these major attractions. The Partnership is supported by a full time community railways officer from the County Council. The Partnership invests in improvements to publicity, minor infrastructure and information at locations away from the railway stations. For further information see www.bitternline.com or email info@norfolk.gov.uk

The Wherry Lines Community Rail Partnership

The Wherry Lines Community Rail Partnership was formed in 2000, following the success of the Bittern Line. Its aims are to promote and grow patronage on the Lowestoft and Great Yarmouth to Norwich local railways. The funding partners are Suffolk County Council, Waveney District Council, Norwich City Council, Norfolk County Council and 'one' railway. Network Rail supports the aims of the Wherry Lines Partnership. The Wherry Lines promote the use of the smallest National Network station at Berney Arms and other small stations along the route in conjunction with the RSPB. The Partnership invests in improvements to publicity, minor infrastructure and information at locations away from the railway stations. For further information please see www.wherrylines.org.uk or email info@norfolk.gov.uk

The Partnership is supported by a full time community railways officer from the County Council.

WAGN

Wagn railway is the main train service provider for the King's Lynn to Cambridge route. We work actively to promote the line and liaise with the local Fen Line Rail Users Group.

We have made considerable investments in this route since privatisation and Downham Market station is now one of our showcase locations.

Additional services have been introduced and the route is growing in popularity which we aim to cater for through further investment.

We have successfully worked with Network Rail and local government to fund continuous improvements along the route and look forward to a bright future working with our strategic partners.

For further information on our trains and service please contact please contact Wagn Customer Relations on 08457 81 89 19 or write to our Customer Relations Manager, Station Road, Cambridge CB1 2JW, email@wagnrail.co.uk www.wagn.co.uk

Widen the Choice

Widen the Choice is a Rural Transport Partnership between the National Trust, the RSPB and The Countryside Agency in the East of England. Its job is to make it easier for people to visit houses, landscapes and nature reserves of the two conservation organisers by means other than by car.

Its aims are to reduce the environmental impact of visitor travel, to improve access to the countryside by more sustainable means of transport, and to promote greater, sustainable use of the countryside and social inclusion.

Our railways are a vital element in this vision. They provide links to RSPB wetland reserves and to houses and countryside of The National Trust in North Norfolk and The Fens, either directly or in conjunction with bus services or cycling. Welcome on board!

ACORP

Founded in 1998, the Association of Community Rail Partnerships (ACoRP) is a national federation of more than fifty local community rail partnerships spread across the United Kingdom.

Community Rail Partnerships are means by which various stakeholders and interested parties along a rail corridor can play an active role in the development of a responsive and good quality rail service. Partnerships bring together train operators, Network Rail, local authorities, community organisations, businesses, development and tourism agencies and other locally based bodies.

ACoRP is a not-for-profit organisation which provides advice and support in developing good quality innovative services on local and rural railways across the United Kingdom.

ACoRP are proud to be a sponsor of 'Iron Roads to the Broads & Fens', we hope that the book brings enjoyment and enlightenment on the best of what our rural and local railways in the East of England can offer.
www.acorp.uk.com

Heinz

Part of the HJ Heinz Company, Heinz Frozen and Chilled Foods Ltd (Westwick) based in Worstead is a £60 million business and one of the UK's leading manufacturers of both frozen Chips and added value Potato Products.

Our extensive brand portfolio includes Aunt Bessie's, Harry Ramsdens and Chip Shop as well as Retailer Own Brands for a number of Major Multiples.

We are pleased to be the official sponsor of Worstead Railway Station and associated with the Bittern Line, which gives many of our employees transport to and from work every day.

The Fen Line Users Association

There was a possibility in the early to mid 80s that the line, now known as The Fen Line, to King's Lynn, might be severed and closed from Ely North Junction. At this point the Borough Council of King's Lynn and West Norfolk desperately tried to do all it could to save it. They also suggested that if the Line could be saved, it should be electrified. It was saved and it was electrified, but at the cost of singling two stretches, one north of Littleport and another north of Downham Market. It was about then, in 1986, that the Association was formed. From 6 direct trains to London from Lynn then, there are 23 today. FLUA continues to strive for train and station facility improvements, whilst it has built up an excellent relationship with all of the Rail Industry, councils - from County to Parish - other organisations, and MPs. It goes from strength to strength.

North Norfolk Railway - The Poppy Line
Live Steam - Living History

The Poppy Line from Sheringham along the coast to Weybourne and up through the heathland to Holt is one of Britain's most scenic heritage steam railways. Originally part of the Midland & Great Northern Railway (affectionately known locally as the Muddle & Get Nowhere), the line is still the perfect epitome of Victorian and Edwardian rural railways, with big, full-size locomotives bringing the age of steam alive.

There are three beautifully restored stations. That at Weybourne, in true railway fashion around a mile from the village it serves, was built in anticipation of the village's development as a resort; but the promoters' dreams were never realised, and the station's real glory days came in serving Weybourne Camp during two world wars. The station at the Holt terminus was originally built by the M&GN at Stalham. Saved and restored by Poppy Line volunteers, a desk in the old booking office still carries the names of the clerks who worked there. The 11-mile round trip on the Poppy Line takes around an hour and a quarter, and all-day hop-on, hop-off Rover tickets allow visitors to explore the places it serves.

The line is supported by the Midland & Great Northern Joint Railway Society, a registered charity. Members receive a quarterly colour magazine and reduced price travel offers. Visit www.mandgn.co.uk for details.

For timetable and special event information, call Sheringham Station on 01263 820800 or visit www.nnr.co.uk

SHERINGHAM • WEYBOURNE • HOLT

Bure Valley Railway

Operating from a junction with the National Rail Network at Wroxham, the railway travels over the nine miles to the market town of Aylsham.

Originally a standard gauge branch from Wroxham opening in 1880, it was taken over by the Great Eastern Railway in 1882. In 1923 it became part of the LNER. Passenger traffic on the line was always sparse and was in danger of withdrawal before WW2. It was saved by the RAF base at Coltishall.

After the war passenger traffic declined and was withdrawn in 1952. Freight continued to be carried until 1982 when the line finally closed. The track was lifted in 1985.

The 15" gauge steam railway was opened in 1990 and has gone from strength to strength. It operates with modern comfortable coaches and a fleet of powerful, purpose-built steam locomotives. The line now carries over 125,000 passengers per year. A real success story.

Photographs

Acknowledgements

The author and publisher extend grateful thanks to Ian Dinmore of Norfolk County Council's Passenger Transport Unit for initially suggesting this guide and for subsequently overseeing its passage from research to completion with discretion and aplomb. Particular thanks must also go to all the organisations who kindly sponsored publication of this book. Several employees of Network Rail have kindly given their time and enthusiasm and they, alphabetically, are Steven & Isla Ashling, Kevin Chapman, David Francis, Chris James and Karen Sinclair. Appreciation also to 'one' Anglia and Central Trains for travel facilities in conjunction with research. Eric Leslie provided the charming Welcome to Wherryland illustration, whilst additional photographs were kindly supplied by Ian Dinmore and Ole Kroczek. We are grateful to Hawksworths of Uttoxeter for organising the printing of this volume and, as always, it would not have materialised at all save for the continued good offices and benedictions displayed by all members of the extended family.